T0345953

Air waves due to a bullet in flight.

The Cambridge Manuals of Science and
Literature

THE PHYSICAL BASIS OF MUSIC

THE PHYSICAL
BASIS OF MUSIC

BY

ALEX. WOOD

M.A. (Cantab.), D.Sc. (Glasgow)

Fellow and Tutor,
Emmanuel College, Cambridge

Cambridge:
at the University Press

1925

CAMBRIDGE UNIVERSITY PRESS
Cambridge, New York, Melbourne, Madrid, Cape Town,
Singapore, São Paulo, Delhi, Mexico City

Cambridge University Press
The Edinburgh Building, Cambridge CB2 8RU, UK

Published in the United States of America by Cambridge University Press, New York

www.cambridge.org
Information on this title: www.cambridge.org/9781107684621

First Edition 1913
Reprinted 1925
First paperback edition 2012

A catalogue record for this publication is available from the British Library

ISBN 978-1-107-68462-1 Paperback

PREFACE

IN the treatment of the subject with which this manual deals very little previous knowledge has been assumed and the author hopes that he has been successful in bringing within the scope of every earnest reader some grasp of the principles. At the same time the subject is no easy one, and the book is not one for an idle half-hour.

In the short bibliography at the end will be found a list of the books to which the author is mainly indebted. In addition he desires to take this opportunity of expressing his special indebtedness to Professor Barton for permission to adapt some tables from his *Text-Book of Sound*, to Messrs Newton and Co. for permission to reproduce the photograph which appears as the frontispiece, to Mr P. W. Wood for reading the proofs and for much helpful criticism, and to the scientific editor of the series for many useful suggestions.

A. W.

December, 1912.

TABLE OF CONTENTS

LIST OF ILLUSTRATIONS

Figs. 21 and 23 are reproduced from the *Encyclopædia Britannica* (11th Edition).

CHAPTER I

THE term "sound" is used in two distinct senses. It is used to denote both the external cause of a particular sensation and that sensation itself. Thus we talk of the production of a sound and the propagation of a sound, referring to particular physical phenomena considered quite apart from any possible hearer, and under the same term we refer to the sensation which these external phenomena produce in ourselves and others.

The sensation of sound is always associated with the vibratory motion of some sounding body. The blurred outline of this body while sounding is sufficient as a rule to convince us of its rapid to-and-fro motion, and, immediately this motion is stopped by a touch of the finger, the sound ceases. Many experiments may be quoted in illustration of this fact. For instance, a moistened finger passed round the rim of a wine-glass or finger-bowl causes it to emit

a strong note. If the surface of the liquid contained
be examined by reflected light, the vibration of the
glass will be found to have revealed itself by throwing
the surface of the liquid into a beautiful pattern
which moves round with the finger. A moment's
thought will convince us that all musical instruments when sounding have vibrating parts—strings,
air-columns, membranes &c.

But, though it is true that our sensation of sound
is always associated with the vibratory motion of a
sounding body, the converse does not always hold.
It is possible to produce vibrations which do not
affect our sense of sound at all. For instance, in the
case of many sounding bodies where the vibrations
die out slowly, it will be found that we cease to hear
the sound before the vibrations have completely
stopped. In this case the energy of the vibrations
has become so small that it is insufficient to set in
action the mechanism of the ear. In order that this
may happen, the energy must be very small indeed.
Thus, in ordinary conversation, the amplitude of
vibration of the layers of air near the ear—that is
the greatest distance which they move in either
direction from their undisturbed position—is always
less than the thousandth part of an inch and often
less than the millionth part of an inch. Sounds
are audible even when the amplitude of the vibrations is 20 or 30 times smaller still. The changes

of pressure produced in the air in the ear may excite the sensation of sound when they are as small as the pressure in the highest vacuum obtainable.

Again, if a card be held in the hand and moved rapidly to and fro, no sound will be heard. This does not mean that the card is in all cases incapable of acting as a source of sound, for, if the edge of the card be touched with the shaft of a vibrating tuning-fork, the volume of sound coming from the fork will be largely increased, the increase being contributed by the vibrations of the card. A good deal of light is thrown on these observations by experiments with a metal strip clamped in a vice. If the end of the strip be pulled aside with the finger and released, it will execute to-and-fro vibrations which will be more rapid the shorter the length of the strip which is free to vibrate. If the strip is taken fairly long at first and then gradually shortened, it will be found that at first its vibrations produce only a feeble whir-ring sound, but that, as the length of the strip is diminished and the vibrations become more rapid, they produce a faint note of low pitch, the pitch rising as the strip is still further shortened. From this we conclude that vibrations may be too slow to affect our sense of sound.

At the other end of the scale a similar phenomenon is found. It may be illustrated by the use of a Galton whistle. This little instrument gives a very high shrill note, and the pitch of the note may be altered continuously by adjusting a stop. If this stop is moved so as to shorten the air-column of the whistle, the vibrations become more and more rapid and the note more and more shrill until suddenly a point is reached at which the note ceases to be heard. The vibrations have not ceased nor have they undergone any sudden change. They have merely become too rapid to affect our sense of sound. The limit varies for different people, becoming lower as a rule with advancing age. Thus we find that the sensation of sound always has its origin in vibration, but that such vibration may be too feeble, too slow or too rapid to produce the sensation.

We now come to consider how the vibrations of a sounding body reach the ear. It is natural to suppose that they are conveyed by some medium, and this is easily verified by experiment. If we exhaust the air from an enclosed space, the vibrations of a bell placed in it fail to excite the sensation of sound. Sound is usually carried by the air, but may also be carried by liquids and solids. A detailed discussion of the way in which the transmission of sound takes place would be out of place here, but some general idea of the process is essential to the right understanding of what follows. One of the most important methods of transmission of energy is by means of waves. All the energy reaching us from the sun—and most of our energy comes from the sun ultimately—is conveyed to us by waves. The energy by which the sensation of sight is excited is transmitted by waves. The energy used for sending wireless messages is carried by waves. The waves with which we are most familiar are no doubt those formed on the surface of water and they may be used to illustrate many important properties of waves, but we get a much clearer idea of the essential feature of wave motion if we think, instead, of the waves which pass across a field of corn under the action of wind. In this case, more perhaps than in any other familiar one, we are brought to realise clearly the distinction between the movement of the waves and the movement of the medium which transmits them. Thus while the wave moves forward, preserving its individuality and to some extent its form, the particular heads of corn whose arrangement gives the wave its form are always changing, being caught up by the front of the wave and then left behind. This is typical of all wave motion. The progressive movement of the wave is always associated with a to-and-fro movement of each part of the medium. The wave is a "form" imposed on the medium and is transmitted without any transference of the medium itself. One of the essential conditions for the propagation of waves is that, when the medium is disturbed, forces should be called into play tending to restore the original undisturbed condition. These forces are supplied in the case under consideration by the elasticity of the corn-stalk, which raises the head again after it has been depressed by the wind. In water waves the principal restoring force is gravity. If a ridge or a hollow is formed on the surface of water, gravity tends to restore the level surface.

We are now in a position to picture to ourselves the propagation through air of waves set up by a vibrating plate. As the plate moves forward, it compresses the layer of air immediately in contact with it. The pressure of the air in this layer is consequently increased. But the layer in front of this again is still at the original pressure. The first layer therefore expands forward into the second in order to equalise the pressure. In doing so it compresses the second layer and this in turn compresses the third, so that a "wave of compression" is propagated outwards with a speed which depends only on the properties of the air and is quite independent of the subsequent motion of the plate. Meantime, the plate having arrived at the end of its forward motion starts backwards again. This gives the layer of air next it additional space to expand into, and the expansion is accompanied by a fall of pressure. This layer is therefore rarefied. But the second layer is still at normal pressure. It therefore expands back into the first layer, itself becoming rarefied. The

third layer expands backwards into the second, and
so a "wave of rarefaction" travels outward after the
wave of compression.

The waves by which sound is propagated are, of
course, ordinarily invisible. This is due to two causes.
In the first place they travel with a speed which,
compared with that of light waves, is extremely small
but, compared with any ordinary standard, is very
great indeed. Thus in air under common atmo-
spheric conditions the waves will travel fully a mile
in five seconds. This is a speed which the eye would
find it impossible to follow. In the second place,
portions of the air differently compressed are not
easy to distinguish although they do exert a slightly
different bending action on rays of light. This is
frequently apparent in hot weather when layers of
heated air which have expanded, and so become less
dense, rise from the hot ground, causing a quivering
of objects seen through them. This phenomenon may
be utilised not only in photographing sound waves,
but even in rendering them visible to the eye. No
matter how rapidly an object may be moving, if it is
illuminated instantaneously, it will be seen distinctly
and apparently at rest. The more rapid its motion,
the shorter must be the duration of the flash which
reveals its presence. By using an electric spark as
the source of light, the waves caused by the passage
of a bullet through the air have been photographed.

The frontispiece is a photograph of a bullet in flight and shows V-shaped air waves spreading out from the front and rear of the bullet respectively. Sound waves, unlike water waves, are not confined to one plane, but spread out in every direction. Thus the waves are at any instant a series of concentric spheres surrounding the source, and not, as in the case of water waves, a series of concentric circles.

In due course these waves arrive at the layer of air in contact with the membrane which closes the inner end of the outer passage of the ear—the so-called "drum" of the ear. This layer is compressed, the layer of air on the inner side of the membrane is still at normal pressure, and so the membrane gets driven inwards. Conversely when the wave of rare-faction arrives, the pressure on the inner side being normal while that on the outer side is less than normal, the membrane gets driven outwards. Thus the motion of the plate is reproduced by the drum of the ear which moves out and in, keeping time with the vibrations of the plate.

Sound waves, like all other waves, experience reflection and refraction. When a series of sea waves wash against a sea wall or esplanade, a series of reflected waves may be seen moving outwards as if they came from behind the reflecting surface. This is of course exactly analogous to the echo; here the sound waves emitted by a source strike a cliff or some similar surface and are reflected back as if they came from a source behind the cliff. Refraction is a phenomenon, equally familiar, in which the waves concerned change their direction of propagation. It occurs whenever the waves move in a medium which is heterogeneous in the sense that some parts of it propagate the waves with greater velocity than others. For instance, in the case of water waves it is a familiar fact that, in whatever direction the waves may be travelling in the deep water, as they approach the shore they change their direction and wheel round, until the length of the wave is practically parallel with the shore. Now this is due to the fact that waves travel faster in deep water than they do in shallow water, and consequently the end of the wave nearer the shore is retarded while the end farther from the shore begins to overtake it, the direction gradually changing as shown in the diagram (Fig. 1).

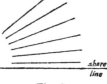

Fig. 1.

Two important examples of the refraction of sound waves occur frequently. So long as the pressure remains the same the velocity of sound waves is greater when the air is less dense and conversely. Consider the case of a hot still day. The layers of air in contact with the ground get heated and expand, thus becoming less dense. It follows that if sound waves are being propagated along the surface of the earth the edges nearest the earth will travel more quickly, and a glance at Fig. 2 will show the effect of this on the direction of propagation of the waves.

It will readily be seen that the direction of propagation soon becomes so much changed that the waves move off into the upper layers of the atmosphere and we have a simple explanation of the well-known fact that under these circumstances

Fig. 2.

sounds carry very badly. Consider now the evening of a day of the same kind. The earth radiates its heat quickly and so cools. It then cools the layers of air in contact with it so that these contract and become more dense. In this case the edges of the

waves next the earth travel more slowly than the upper portions of the waves so that the direction changes as in Fig. 3, the waves being directed down towards the surface of the earth instead of moving off into the atmosphere. This explains

Fig. 3.

the great distinctness with which sounds frequently carry in the evening of a hot day—a distinctness which is of course all the greater over a smooth surface, for instance a sheet of water.

A very similar phenomenon is the propagation of sound with and against the wind. Remembering that the layers of air in contact with the ground will be retarded by friction and so will move less quickly than higher layers we see that if the waves are travelling with the wind the upper edges will move more rapidly and we shall have very much the state of things represented in Fig. 3, while if the waves are travelling against the wind we shall have the conditions represented in Fig. 2. Thus the fact, that sound carries much better with the wind than against it, is satisfactorily accounted for.

Of the large variety of sounds which affect our ears only a certain proportion have any musical value. The others are mere noises. If we try to analyse the sensations which we classify as notes or as noises we shall find that as a rule the sensation of a musical note is smooth, regular and of definite pitch. Noises on the other hand are sensations irregular and discontinuous. This distinction can be illustrated practically by means of a useful little instrument devised by Koenig and known as the manometric flame. Two saucer-shaped pieces of wood or metal are fixed with their rims in contact and the chamber so formed is divided into two parts by a flexible membrane (see Fig. 4). Into the right-hand division of the chamber a single wide tube A is led ; while into the left hand division two tubes B and C are led. If now

B is connected to a small gas-jet and C to the gas supply it will be obvious that so long as the membrane remains at rest the jet will burn with a steady flame. Any motion of the membrane, however, will at once affect the height of the flame which will be greater when the membrane is moving towards the left and less when the membrane moves towards the right.

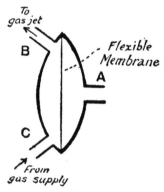

Fig. 4.

Obviously then, if the tube A is directed towards a source of sound the arrival of successive compressions and rarefactions at the membrane will cause it to move and this motion will be communicated to the flame which will move up and down in time with the impulses arriving at the membrane. There still remains one serious obstacle in the way of using

the motion of the flame as an indicator of what is
happening in the sound waves. In an ordinary musical
note compressions and rarefactions succeed one
another several hundreds of times per second and if
the flame moves up and down with this frequency it
will be quite impossible to detect any motion at all.
If a note is sung into the tube A and the flame
carefully observed, no trace of motion will be seen.
An ingenious device is used to overcome this difficulty. If a mirror be made to rotate rapidly in the
neighbourhood of the flame, and if, instead of ob-
serving the flame directly, we observe its image in
the rotating mirror its motion will be revealed. As
the mirror rotates about a vertical axis the image
of the flame will appear to move across its surface
and if the flame is always of the same size the image
will be always the same height and so the bright
band which it shows in the mirror will have a smooth
upper surface. On the other hand if the flame is
moving rapidly up and down, the upper edge of the
bright band in the mirror will be serrated and the
character of this serration is capable of giving us
much useful information as to the nature of the
sound which is causing it. It is found that when
A is directed towards a "noise" the serrations are
entirely irregular, while a musical note produces
serrations all similar and equally spaced.

At the same time no hard and fast line can be

drawn between the two classes of sounds. Almost all notes are accompanied by noises and many noises have some of the characteristics of a musical note— e.g. pitch. A little practice will enable anyone with a sense of pitch to assign a definite pitch to such noises as are made for instance by a piece of firewood allowed to fall on the hearth, or by the drawing of a cork.

It is found that all the notes used in music are associated with regular periodic motion—that is, a motion which continually repeats itself and always in the same time. The motion of the bob of a pendulum is periodic, so is the motion of the prong of a tuning-fork. In both cases the point on which we fix our attention describes the same path again and again, and always completes it in the same interval of time— an interval which is known as its *period*. If for instance we take the plate on which we based our discussion on page 6, and fix it to some mechanism capable of giving it a rapid and regular to-and-fro motion it will emit a musical note. The to-and-fro motion may be extremely complicated. The plate may move rapidly at some points of its path and slowly at others, may sometimes partially retrace its steps—these eccentricities will affect the character of the sound to some extent but if the vibration of the plate, however complicated, is regularly repeated in equal intervals of time it will emit a musical note.

The motion of the drum of the ear will of course also be periodic and will have the same period as the vibrating plate. The number of complete vibrations executed per second by a vibrating body is called the *frequency* of its vibration. The maximum displacement of the vibrating body from its undisturbed position is called the *amplitude* of its vibration. It is important to notice that while the frequency of vibration of the drum of the ear, of the intervening layers of air and of the source of sound are all the same, the amplitudes of the layers of air fall off with increasing distance from the source until the drum of the ear is reached—its amplitude consequently being in general much smaller than that of the source of sound.

CHAPTER II

DISTINGUISHING CHARACTERISTICS OF MUSICAL NOTES

MUSICAL notes may be distinguished from each other by three characteristics—loudness, pitch and quality (or *timbre*). Our common experience will to some extent have prepared us for the discovery that loudness depends on the amplitude of vibration of the membrane of the ear and therefore, other things being equal, on the amplitude of the vibration of the sounding body. If a tuning-fork is forcibly struck the sound emitted is strong at first but gradually dies away as the vibrations diminish in amplitude. Looking at the matter from a slightly different point of view, we may say that the loudness of a particular sound depends on the rate at which the ear is receiving energy from the source of sound. This, for a given sound, depends immediately on the amplitude of vibration of the air in the ear and so ultimately on the amplitude of the vibrating body. This view is more helpful when we come to consider a very important principle recognised in almost all musical instruments. If a tuning-fork be held in the air after being struck, the sound emitted is hardly perceptible, but if it is placed with its handle resting on a wooden table the sound immediately swells out. This is not due to any increase of the amplitude of vibration of the fork but to the fact that it now communicates its vibrations to the table and so the whole surface of the table is made to vibrate in unison with the fork. The table, being in contact with a large mass of air, sets that vibrating and in so doing communicates energy to it. But the source of all this energy is the initial blow given to the fork, the effect of the table being to increase the rate at which the fork parts with its energy. Thus more energy is received at the ear per second and this increase in the rate at which energy is received by the ear accounts for the increased loudness of the sound. If this explanation is the true one, it follows that the fork will remain sounding much longer if held in the air than if allowed to touch the table. This will be found to be the case. If the fork be struck as nearly as possible with the same force in the two cases, its initial store of energy will be the same, but will be much less rapidly exhausted in the first case than in the second. This phenomenon is of the greatest importance in the construction of musical instruments. In many cases the primary source of the note has so small a surface area that it communicates energy to the air only very slowly and consequently gives rise to a very feeble sound. Where the surface is narrow, as in the case of a small tuning-fork, there is very considerable lateral motion of the air, which passes backwards and forwards round the prongs without ever being appreciably compressed or rarefied at all. This may be demonstrated by a simple experiment due to Sir George Stokes. If a card is held close to one prong of a tuning-fork while the fork is sounding in air, in such a way as to obstruct this lateral motion, the loudness of the sound emitted by the fork will be considerably increased. In an even greater degree is this true of a vibrating string. If a string be stretched between two quite rigid supports and plucked, hardly any sound is perceptible.

The sound produced by a piano or a violin is due to the fact that, associated with the string are large surfaces—the sounding board of the piano and the body of the violin—which take up the vibrations of the string and virtually increase its vibrating surface. Sometimes a column of air is used for a similar purpose. The air contained in the box on which a tuning-fork is frequently mounted plays this part, and in the case of brass wind instruments the lips of the performer are usually the primary source of sound, but this otherwise feeble sound is reinforced by the vibrations of the column of air in the instrument. This case is different from the others previously cited, in that, while the sounding board of a piano will reinforce every note of the scale, the column of air in a bugle will only reinforce a very limited series. This difference will be dealt with subsequently.

Musical notes are distinguished from one another not only by loudness but also by pitch. The discovery of the characteristic of the external vibration which corresponds to pitch presents little difficulty. We have all noticed, when running our finger-nails down corded silk, that a note of quite definite pitch is emitted. We may also have noticed that the pitch depends on the speed with which the nail is moved over the silk. If this is done very slowly we hear the separate taps of the nail on the ridges of the silk, but as the motion is made more rapid we get instead a note of higher and higher pitch. This at once suggests that the sensation of pitch depends on the frequency with which the impulses due to the separate taps succeed one another at the ear.

The principle may be tested by means of an instrument known as the siren. In its simplest form it consists of a circular cardboard or metal disk mounted on an axle. The disk is perforated with a ring of equi-distant holes. When the disk is rotated the perforations come successively in front of a nozzle from which issues a blast of air. Thus the air comes through the perforations in a series of puffs which succeed one another more or less rapidly according to the speed of rotation of the disk. If the number of perforations in the ring be known and the number of revolutions which the disk makes in a second be also known, the number of puffs issuing per second can be easily calculated. As we should expect, if the rate at which the puffs are emitted be very slow the ear perceives them separately, but as the speed of rotation is increased the puffs begin to fuse into one continuous sound of low pitch. Further increase of speed causes a steady rise in the pitch of the resulting note. The sound emitted by a siren of this kind is very feeble and the instrument has been much improved. In the later forms a wind-chest takes the place of the tube conveying the air blast, and the disk is made to rotate close to the upper surface of

the wind-chest. This surface is perforated to correspond with the perforations of the disk, so that
each time one of the holes on the top of the wind-
chest coincides in position with one of the holes in
the disk all the holes in both coincide and a puff of
air comes simultaneously through each pair of coincident holes. This greatly strengthens the sound.
A very interesting and important fact which may be
verified by means of the siren is, that the pitch of a
note depends only on the number of impulses reaching
the ear per second and not at all on the way in which
these impulses are produced. Thus if a quill be held
so that it strikes the holes of the revolving disk it will
be found that it gives rise to a note of the same pitch
as is produced by the air puffs for the same speed of
rotation. Or again, if a toothed wheel be made to
rotate and a card or metal strip be held against it,
a note of definite pitch will be emitted. The pitch
will be the same as that of the note given by the
siren if the frequency of the impacts of the card on
the teeth of the revolving wheel be the same as the
frequency of the air puffs given by the siren.

The siren is very useful for enabling us to
determine the frequency of vibration corresponding
to any particular note. Thus, in order to determine
the frequency of a tuning-fork, we cause it to sound
and adjust the speed of rotation of the disk of the
siren until the note given by the siren is in unison

with the fork. Keeping the unison as perfect as possible we count the number of revolutions which the disk of the siren makes in a given time, and then, knowing the number of perforations in the disk, we are able to calculate the number of puffs emitted per second. This will be the number of vibrations made by the fork per second. Thus suppose we keep the fork and the siren in unison for 30 seconds and that during that time the counting apparatus shows that the disk has revolved 320 times; suppose further that we count the number of holes in the disk and find it to be 24; then the total number of air puffs emitted is 24×320 or 7680. The number per second is therefore this number divided by 30, that is 256. This last number then is the frequency of the fork. Some of the more interesting frequencies are given below. Here and elsewhere throughout the text we shall use Helmholtz' notation—see Table I at the end of this volume.

$C_{,,}$	Lowest tone of very large organs	16·5
$A_{,,}$	Lowest tone of very large pianos	27·5
$C_{,}$	Usual lower limit	33
a'	From Handel's Fork, 1751	422·5
a'	Erard's Concert Pitch, 1879	455·3
a^{iv}	Usual highest tone of large pianos ...	3,520
d^{v}	Highest tone of piccolo flute	4,752
e^{viii}	Highest tone reached (Appun and Preyer's tuning-fork)	40,960

The determination of the upper and lower limits of audibility, especially the latter, has been the subject of much controversy, but it may be safely asserted that our ears are sensitive to sounds having frequencies lying between about 30 vibrations per second and 40,000 vibrations per second, but that the frequencies of sounds having any real musical value lie between about 40 and 4000.

An interesting phenomenon bearing on the relation between pitch and frequency is the apparent alteration in pitch of a note due to the relative motion of the source and the observer. An observer standing in a railway station while an express train passes through whistling can hardly fail to be struck with the sudden drop in pitch of the note given by the whistle just as the engine passes. Often, on the road, the approach of a motor car at high speed is indicated by a hum of very definite pitch and in this case also the drop in pitch as the car passes is very noticeable. In order to understand this we have only to realise that as the source of sound approaches us the sound waves which it emits get crowded up into smaller space. Between the instant when one compression is sent out and the instant when it is followed by the next the source of sound has moved forward so that these two compressions travel outwards separated by less than their natural distance apart. Hence the compressions sent out by the source arrive at the ear in quicker succession than would be the case if source and observer were relatively at rest. The converse happens when the source of sound is receding from the observer. Here the compressions succeed one another at the ear less rapidly than would be the case if the source were at rest. Thus in the first case the apparent pitch is higher than the true pitch while in the latter case it is lower[1].

The siren may be used to investigate the frequency relations between two notes constituting a simple musical interval. For experiments of this kind a further development of the siren is found convenient. In this form there are four concentric rings of holes in the wind-chest and revolving disk—each ring having a different number of holes. A convenient arrangement is that in which the numbers of holes in successive rings are in the ratios 4, 5, 6, 8. The apparatus is arranged so that the various rings may be opened or shut at will. Now we know that there are certain pairs of notes which our ears at once recognise as standing to one another in some simple relationship. The most familiar case is the octave. If a note and its octave are sounded successively the observer instinctively feels that the two notes are related. If we open successively the first and last rings of holes in our siren while the disk is rotating, we shall find that the note given by the last is the octave above that given by the first. Moreover, this remains true for all speeds of rotation, so that we

[1] Known as Dӧpplers Principle.

are driven to conclude that, whatever may be the
frequency of a given note, its octave will always have
a frequency twice as great. If we experiment next
with the first and third rings we find that the latter
gives a note a Fifth above that given by the former.
This also holds for all speeds of rotation so that we
see that when two notes are a musical Fifth apart
their frequencies must be in the ratio of 6 to 4,
i.e. 3 to 2. The various musical intervals are named
—or numbered—by counting up the scale from one
note to another and including both the note we count
from and the note we count to. Thus C to D is the
Second, C to E is the Third, C to F is the Fourth,
and so on. It is found, when we compare the frequencies, that E to G is a smaller interval than C
to E. It is therefore called a Minor Third while C
to E is called a Major Third. In the same way we
have two kinds of Sixths, Major and Minor. We
shall find that, by utilising different pairs, the four
rows of holes in the disk of our siren will give us the
Octave, Fifth, Fourth, Major Third, Minor Third and
Minor Sixth. Other intervals may be obtained by
using a siren disk in which the numbers of holes are
in a different ratio. The results of investigations of
this kind are tabulated in Table II (see end of volume)
where the notes forming the interval are given as
well as the ratio of the frequencies. The first thing
that strikes us on a glance at the Table is that it

includes all the simplest and most harmonious intervals and that in all cases the frequencies of the notes forming the interval are in a ratio which may be expressed by two small whole numbers. It will also be seen on comparing the Minor Sixth with the Fifth and the Octave that the simpler the interval the smaller are the two numbers in terms of which the ratio of the frequencies of the notes may be expressed. We are here using the word simple as an indication of the ease with which the interval in question may be recognised and picked out by the ear, and it is well known that in this respect the Octave, Fifth, and Fourth come before the Sixths and Thirds. The explanation of these simple ratios will become clear later and meanwhile it is sufficient to call attention to the fact.

We are now in a position to determine the relative frequencies of all the notes of the scale, so that if the frequency of one be given we can calculate all the others. Thus we see from Table II that, whatever may be the frequency of C, the frequency of c must be twice as great. Considering the interval of the Fifth we see that whatever be the frequency of C that of G must be 3/2 times as great. Thus if we start with C as 1 then the Octave gives us c as 2, the Major Sixth gives us A as 5/3, the Fifth gives us G as 3/2, the Fourth gives us F as 4/3, the Major Third gives us E as 5/4. The corresponding ratio for D

may be got by noticing among the Fourths that it is
the Fourth *below* G.   It must therefore be

$$3/4 \times 3/2 = 9/8.$$

In the same way it will be seen that B is a Fifth
above E and must therefore have the ratio

$$3/2 \times 5/4 = 15/8.$$

Thus we now have the following series of ratios

C	D	E	F	G	A	B	c
1	9/8	5/4	4/3	3/2	5/3	15/8	2

We can clear of fractions by taking C as 24, in which
case the scale becomes

C	D	E	F	G	A	B	c
24	27	30	32	36	40	45	48

Remembering that the size of the interval between two notes is always measured by the *ratio* of
the two frequencies, we can obtain the intervals
between the successive notes of the scale by dividing
the number representing each note by the number
representing the one immediately below. Thus the
interval from C to D is given by the ratio 27/24,
or 9/8. Similarly the interval from D to E is given
by the ratio 30/27, which simplifies to 10/9. Carrying
out this process for the whole scale we obtain the
following ratios as representing the intervals between successive notes,

C	D	E	F	G	A	B	c
	9/8	10/9	16/15	9/8	10/9	9/8	16/15

It will be seen that these intervals are of three different sizes, the largest ratio is 9/8 and the interval so measured is called a Large Tone. Next to it, and not very different from it is the interval whose ratio is 10/9 which is called a Small Tone and last of all and much smaller is the interval whose ratio is 16/15 which is called a Semitone. Now this matter of measuring intervals by ratios is somewhat of a stumbling-block to the uninitiated. For instance it is hard for a mind unaccustomed to working with ratios to form any idea of the comparative sizes of the Tone and Semitone simply by looking at the ratios which define these intervals. A further difficulty is that in adding two intervals we have to multiply the corresponding ratios. Thus the interval obtained by adding a Fifth and a Fourth is represented by the ratio $3/2 \times 4/3 = 2$, so that a Fifth added to a Fourth gives us an Octave, as we know to be the case. In order to evade this and similar difficulties, the intervals are measured by logarithms in the manner shown in the Appendix. In the system most generally adopted the Octave is divided into twelve hundred equal parts called cents. In terms of these cents we get the following values for the various familiar intervals.

Octave	...	1200	Major Third	386
Major Sixth		884	Minor Third	316
Minor Sixth		814	Major Tone	204
Fifth	...	702	Minor Tone	182
Fourth	...	498	Semitone ...	112

These numbers enable us to compare the different intervals by simply adding and subtracting. Thus we see that a Fifth plus a Fourth gives us

$$702 + 498 = 1200 = \text{Octave}.$$

For convenience of reference most of this information is collected in Table III as we shall find it very necessary to have it accessible while reading the later chapters. It is perhaps well that the reader should be warned at this point that the scale for which the above calculations hold exactly is an ideal one, from which it is found necessary to depart in actual practice for reasons which will be discussed in the chapter on Temperament. Thus the tuning of the white notes of the piano only approximately follows the numbers here given.

And now we must pass on to consider the third characteristic of the musical note—quality. Like pitch and many other quite familiar ideas it is somewhat hard to define. It is the property which enables us to distinguish between two notes of the same pitch and the same loudness when produced by different kinds of instruments or even by two different voices. This will be found to depend on the kind of vibration which is giving rise to the note. The sounding body may for instance have a simple to-and-fro motion like that of the bob of a pendulum, fast at the middle of its range and slow at both ends.

On the other hand it may move with uniform speed
from end to end of its range, experiencing a sudden
change of speed just at each end. The prong of a
tuning-fork has a vibration of the first kind while a
point on a violin string when the string is being bowed
is found to have a vibration approximating to the
second kind. It is very desirable to have some method
of representing graphically the various possible types
of vibration and in order to do this recourse is
had to what is called the displacement diagram of
the vibrating point. Suppose for instance that we
have a pencil point in contact with a vertical sheet
of paper and that we make the pencil point move up
and down vertically. It will trace out a vertical
straight line on the paper which will give us no
information at all about its motion. Suppose however that while the pencil is moving up and down
the paper is drawn steadily from left to right. The
pencil will now trace a wavy curve on the paper
from which much information may be gathered.
We know that had the paper been at rest while
the pencil moved we should have had a vertical line,
and on the other hand if the paper had moved and
the pencil been kept at rest we should have had a
horizontal line. The line we have actually obtained
is the resultant of the two motions and it follows
that where the pencil has been moving relatively
slowly the curve will be nearly horizontal, while

where it has been moving relatively rapidly the
curve will approach the vertical. A trace of this
kind, whether drawn directly by the vibrating body,
as in the case mentioned, or drawn from observations
and measurements of the motion, is called the displacement diagram of the vibrating point. Below
are shown some typical displacement diagrams.

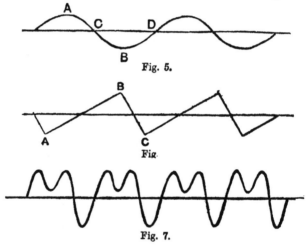

Fig. 5.

Fig.

Fig. 7.

Fig. 5 represents the motion of a pendulum bob.
It would be produced if the pendulum bob terminated
in a pencil and were made to vibrate across a sheet
of paper while the sheet was drawn sideways. We
see that at *A* and *B* the line is parallel to the

direction in which the paper is being drawn so that
at these points the bob of the pendulum must be
momentarily at rest. At C and D on the other hand
the line is steepest so that these must be the points
of most rapid motion. Thus the curve reveals the
fact that the pendulum bob is moving most rapidly
at the centre of its range, slows up towards both
ends and just at either end is momentarily at rest.
This type of motion is very important and is known
as simple harmonic motion. Fig. 6 is the displacement diagram for a point on a violin string. The
straight lines show that the speed of the point
remains constant from end to end of its range,
being suddenly changed at each end. The fact that
the two straight lines AB and BC which together
represent a complete vibration of the point are not
equally steep, indicates that the point moves faster
in one direction than it does on the return journey.
Many displacement diagrams are of course much
more complicated. In some cases, as was suggested
earlier, the vibrating point actually partially retraces
its path. A simple example of this kind is given in
Fig. 7. If a pencil be made to trace out this curve
by moving up and down the page while the page
itself is drawn from right to left, the pencil point
will execute the vibration which the displacement
diagram represents.

If a very narrow slit be cut in a sheet of stiff

writing paper and placed with its length parallel to
the side of the page near the left-hand side of one of
these displacement diagrams, the intersection of the
curve with the slit will show as a black dot. If now
the sheet of paper be drawn steadily from left to
right this black dot will move up and down the slit
with the motion which the displacement diagram is
drawn to represent. The characteristics mentioned
in the text will be clearly shown.

CHAPTER III

INTERFERENCE OF WAVES.   STATIONARY
VIBRATION

ONE of the most characteristic phenomena associated with wave motion of all kinds is what has come
to be known as "interference." The discoverer of
the phenomenon was Thomas Young, of Emmanuel
College, Cambridge, and it was probably suggested
to his mind first of all in connection with water
waves.   His application of the principle to optical
phenomena did much to establish the fact that light
is propagated by some kind of wave motion.   In one
of his papers he thus describes the phenomenon.
"Suppose a number of equal waves of water to move
upon the surface of a stagnant lake, with a certain

velocity, and to enter a narrow channel leading out
of the lake. Suppose then another similar cause to
have excited another equal series of waves, which
arrive at the same channel with the same velocity
and at the same time with the first. Neither series
of waves will destroy the other, but their effects will
be combined: if they enter the channel in such a
manner that the elevations of the one series coincide
with those of the other, they must together produce
a series of greater joint elevations ; but if the elevations of one series are so situated as to correspond to
the depressions of the other, they must exactly fill up
those depressions, and the surface of the water must
remain smooth." It is the latter case which makes
the strongest appeal to the imagination and no
doubt this fact is responsible for the application of
the term "interference" to the phenomenon. Not only
could we produce in our observation channel either
smooth water or a series of waves of double height,
but by suitably altering the conditions we could produce a system of waves which would have any height
between these extremes. Taking a broad view of the
phenomenon in all its aspects, we see that the principle
simply involves a statement of the fact that when
any point in a medium is influenced simultaneously
by two independent wave systems, its displacement
at any instant is the sum or difference of the displacements, which each system would separately have

produced, according as these displacements are in the same or in opposite directions. That is to say, if at any instant the particle under consideration would have been on the crest of a wave belonging to one system and in the trough of a wave belonging to the other system, then if the two systems have waves of equal heights the particle will simply remain undisplaced. Thus each wave system makes its own contribution to the motion of the area which is traversed by both and, when it has emerged from the area common to both, proceeds exactly as it would have done had the other system never been present. If these facts are unfamiliar to us in the case of water waves it is not for lack of opportunity to observe them. Every sheet of water frequently presents them to our notice. There we can see the system of waves or ripples due to the wind moving steadily in one direction and, perhaps, a circular system spreading out from a spot where a stone has been thrown in. Each system preserves its own identity and moves exactly as if the other were not present. Often we can see the V-shaped system due to a moving boat passing out and through the wind system, while on occasion these may even chance to be combined with a third system, and we shall find that what holds for two systems holds equally for any number. We are in a position now to realise that "interference" is an unfortunate term for the phenomenon. We see that each system moves on without interfering with any other, and without interference from any other, although it may happen that at certain points the two or more independent motions may combine to produce rest. A very familiar case of "interference" of sound waves is afforded by a tuning-fork. Obviously while the prongs are moving outwards compressions are started in front of the prongs and propagated outwards in the direction in which the prongs are moving. On the other hand a rarefaction will be formed between the prongs and this will be propagated out sideways, at right angles to the direction of motion of the prongs. Thus if figure 8 represents the plan of the fork we have compressions propagated along AB and AC and rarefactions along AD and AE. It follows that somewhere, approximately in directions bisecting the right angles between these four directions, the compressions and rarefactions must combine to give normal pressure. The converse will happen when the prongs are moving inwards. In this case compressions will travel outwards along AD and AE and rarefactions along AB and AC, but it will still be true that along the directions AF, AG, AH, AK, the compressions and rarefactions will combine to give normal pressure. Thus along the directions AB, AC, AD, AE, there travel successively compressions and rarefactions which will affect the ear, while along four directions between these the pressure does not vary. It follows that as the tuning-fork is slowly rotated close to the ear the sound will swell and diminish four times in each revolution of the fork—a result which may be readily verified.

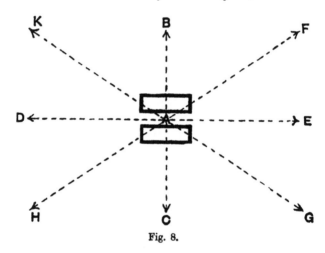

Fig. 8.

In order to get anything like a complete view of the phenomenon of interference we must return to the consideration of displacement diagrams. Let it be borne in mind that, when a medium is transmitting waves, each small portion of the medium exactly repeats the motion of its immediate neighbour a small fraction of time later. It follows that

any diagram which represents the displacements of a
portion of the medium at successive instants will
also represent the displacement of successive portions
of the medium at any given instant.   If for instance
we consider a diagram like Fig. 9, one of the broken
lines may be the displacement diagram for a drop on
the surface of a sheet of water which is transmitting
waves.   In that case the successive ordinates Aa_1,
Bb_1, Cc_1 and so on represent the displacements of
the drop at successive instants.   But the diagram

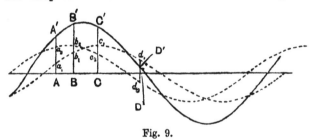

Fig. 9.

representing the displacements of successive drops
at any instant would have exactly the same form,
since the other drops in the line of propagation of
the waves are all executing the same vibration and,
at the instant in question, each shows a different
stage of it.   Thus the broken line may be taken to
represent the form of the water surface at any
particular instant, due to a system of waves.   Now
let the other broken line represent the form which

would have been impressed on the water surface
by another system at the same instant had the first
system been absent. If these two systems act simultaneously we shall get the resultant displacement of
successive drops on the surface of the water by
drawing at various points the ordinates $A a_1 a_2$, $B b_1 b_2$,
$C c_1 c_2$, $D d_1 d_2$ and marking off on them A', B', C', D',
making $A A' = A a_1 + A a_2$, $B B' = B b_1 + B b_2$ and so
on. Where the displacements are opposite as at
D the two ordinates must be subtracted so that
$D D' = D d_1 - D d_2$. If this construction is carried

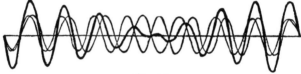

Fig. 10.

out for each point and then the resulting points
A', B', C', D' &c. joined by a smooth curve, we shall
get the displacement diagram representing the united
effect of the two separate systems. This is shown
in the diagram by the continuous line. In Fig. 10
is shown the result of combining two waves of equal
amplitude and nearly equal wave length. Now
this method is perfectly general and can be applied
at once to the case of any kind of waves. For
instance we have seen that when layers of air are

transmitting sound waves they move to and fro in the direction in which the waves are travelling and not up and down at right angles to that direction, as in the case of the drops of water when waves are passing along the surface. It is true that in the case of air waves the displacement diagram does not give such an accurate picture of the state of the medium; but if we adopt the convention that forward displacements of the layers of air are to be repre-

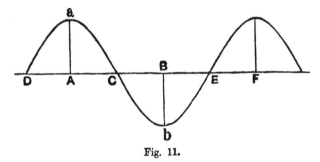

Fig. 11.

sented by lines drawn upwards from the axis of the diagram and backward displacements by lines drawn downwards, we shall then obtain displacement diagrams exactly like those we have been dealing with and shall be able to interpret them so as to ascertain what is happening to the various layers of air. Suppose for instance that Fig. 11 represents the state at a particular instant of air transmitting waves from left to right. We see that the layer of air whose undisturbed position is A, is at the instant under consideration displaced forwards through a distance $= Aa$. The layer at C is undisplaced, while the layer whose normal position is B is displaced backwards through a distance $= Bb$. Intermediate layers are displaced by intermediate amounts. We also notice that the layers between D and C are displaced forwards, while the layers between E and C are displaced backwards. There must therefore be a crowding of the layers and so a compression at C. On the other hand, fixing our attention on E we see that the layers between E and C are displaced backwards, while those between E and F are displaced forwards. Therefore on both sides of E the layers of air are displaced away from it so that we shall have a rarefaction at E. Wherever then the displacement diagram cuts the axis, passing downwards in the direction of propagation of the waves, we have a compression; while where it crosses the axis upwards in the same direction we have a rarefaction. We also see that as the crest of the wave, represented by a, moves forward from left to right, lines drawn upwards from points on the axis between A and C to meet the curve would all become longer. Now the lengths of these lines represent the forward displacements of the corresponding layers of air. These layers are therefore increasing their forward displacements—i.e. are moving forwards. On the other hand downward drawn lines from points between *B* and *C* to the curve would get shorter. This means that the backward displacement of the corresponding layers of air is getting less—i.e. these layers also are moving forward. Thus all the layers of air forming the compression are moving forwards. A similar discussion of the motion of layers of air corresponding to points between *B* and *F*—i.e. to the rarefaction—shows them to be moving backwards. It is important to distinguish between displacement and motion. Thus at the instant in question layers between *B* and *C* are displaced *backwards* but are moving *forwards*. It follows from this that we can obtain the resultant effect of a series of waves passing through the air in exactly the same way as we have indicated for water waves. The application of Fig. 10 to air waves is particularly interesting and important. It represents the case of sound coming from two sources of nearly but not quite the same pitch. The one of higher pitch will send out compressions and rarefactions at slightly shorter intervals and so will have a slightly shorter wave-length. The resultant effect of the two wave systems is, that instead of a series of uniform waves, which would produce at the ear a steady note, we get a series of waves whose amplitude alternately increases and diminishes so that the sound alternately swells and lulls. If the two separate

wave systems have the same amplitudes, the amplitude
of the resultant wave system will sink to zero between
each consecutive pair of maxima and the resultant
sound will, at the corresponding instants, disappear
altogether.   This phenomenon is well known in
acoustics.   If we take two tuning-forks of the same
pitch and load the prongs of one with a little wax so
as to diminish its frequency and lower its pitch, we
shall find that if they are made to sound together
we get very marked alternate swells and lulls of the
sound.   The phenomenon is known as beating.   Suppose that the loaded fork now makes one vibration
less in each second than the unloaded one, and suppose
further that we start our consideration of the phenomenon when they are vibrating in the same phase
—i.e. they send out their compressions together and
their rarefactions together ; these will travel to the
ear and simultaneously produce their effects on the
membrane which will thus have imparted to it a
double amplitude of vibration—assuming the amplitudes of the two forks to be equal.   Thus the ear will
hear a loud sound.   But one of the forks is gradually
gaining on the other and after half a second it will
have gained half a vibration so that now when one
fork sends out a compression the other sends out
a rarefaction at the same instant and vice versa.
Consequently a compression from one fork reaches
the ear simultaneously with a rarefaction from the

other, the two annul one another, the membrane of
the ear does not move, and no sound is heard,
although both forks are still sounding strongly. The
fork of greater frequency still continues to gain and
at the end of the second has gained a complete
vibration and once more the conditions existing at
the beginning of the second are repeated. Thus we
have a succession of beats occurring regularly once a
second. In order to have periods of absolute silence
it is necessary that the two amplitudes should be
the same—a condition difficult to ensure—but if the
amplitudes are even nearly the same the beating
will be very marked. Beats have several important
applications in music. They enable us to achieve
very great accuracy in tuning two notes to unison.
If the two notes are at all close in pitch beats will
be heard. One of the notes is then slightly altered.
If the beating is rendered slower, unison is being
approached and the note is further altered in the
same direction until the beating finally disappears.
From what has been said it will be obvious that the
number of beats per second given by two notes is
equal to the number of whole vibrations which the
one will gain on the other in one second, and is
therefore equal to the difference of frequencies. The
slow beating due to imperfect tuning is usually considered rather pleasing and is intentionally utilised
in the Vox Humana stop of the organ which brings

into play a series of imperfectly tuned pairs of pipes.

We have seen that, when waves are being propagated through a medium, each particle taking part in the motion repeats the motion of its neighbour an instant later. It executes an exactly similar orbit in the same period of time. There is however another type of vibration known as "stationary vibration" which differs from this in several important respects. In this case each particle vibrates with an amplitude either greater or less than that of its neighbour—the medium being divided up into regions of maximum motion and regions of minimum motion, these regions succeeding one another at equal intervals. One of the simplest illustrations of this type of vibration is given by a rope or rubber cord. If one end of the cord be fixed to a hook and the other held in the hand, a quick motion of the hand will be found to send a pulse along the cord and the pulse will be reflected from the fixed end and will travel back again to the hand. By giving the hand a properly timed to-and-fro motion it will be found possible to get the whole string to vibrate together. This is a typical case of stationary vibration. The two ends are points of minimum motion, the centre is a point of maximum motion. The former points are called nodes, the latter point is called a loop, and the division of a medium into loops and nodes is characteristic of stationary vibration.

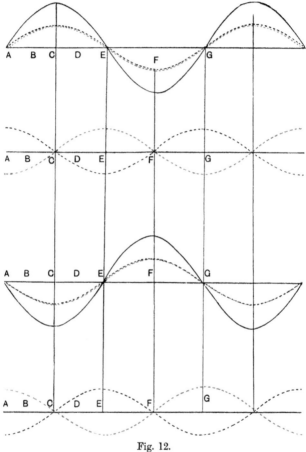

Fig. 12.

Stationary Vibration.

If the hand be now moved to and fro with a frequency twice as great, the cord will be found to split up into two vibrating portions or loops, separated by a comparatively stationary point or node at the centre. Increasing the frequency still further we find it possible to make the cord break up into three loops and so on. It is a little difficult at first to get the timing of the hand sufficiently accurate to give the string a steady motion, but a little practice is all that is necessary. Some clue to the way in which these loops and nodes are produced is given by the fact that we are really dealing with two systems of waves—one, the direct system, sent along by the hand, and the other the reflected system travelling back again from the fixed end. If we apply the method of superposition to the displacement diagrams for the two systems we shall find it gives us the complete solution of the problem. Let the red and black dotted lines (Fig. 12) represent two systems of waves, equal in amplitude and wave-length, the system represented by the black line moving from right to left and that represented by the red line from left to right. Then the continuous line represents the resultant effect on the medium. The condition of the medium is shown at four successive instants. At the first of these the two systems are acting together so that the displacement of each point of the medium is double what it would have been had

either system been acting alone. At the second
instant considered, the two wave systems have moved
through a quarter of a wave-length to left and right
respectively, and now oppose one another at all points.
At the third instant they have again moved to left
and right through a quarter wave-length and are once
more acting together. In the fourth instant shown
they are once more in opposition. Thus we see that
the medium is alternately undisplaced and subject to
double displacement. Let us now fix our attention
on the portions of the medium represented by the
points A, B, C, D, E, F. It will be seen that A and
E are never displaced at all while C and F are
displaced alternately in opposite directions, their
maximum displacements being the sum of the amplitudes of the two constituent wave systems. Thus
A and E are nodes while C and F are loops, and we
have the conditions of stationary vibration. B and
D have vibrations whose amplitudes are less than
those of C and F. Indeed it will be seen that the
points from A to C have vibrations of gradually
increasing amplitude, while in passing from C to E
the amplitudes diminish again to zero. This distribution of amplitudes is repeated again between E and
G. It will also be noticed that at any instant the displacement of consecutive loops is opposite in direction.

If the waves with which we are dealing are transverse waves—that is, if the vibrations of the particles

of the medium which transmits the waves are at right angles to the direction in which the waves are travelling—then the displacement diagram we have obtained gives a very exact representation of what is happening. This is of course true for the waves travelling along the cord, as in this case the vibrations of each small portion of the cord are at right angles to the length of the cord. Nevertheless the discussion applies equally well to air waves if we use the convention already mentioned (p. 39) as to the way in which forward and backward displacements are to be represented. The practical application of these results to the vibrating parts of musical instruments is given in the next chapter.

CHAPTER IV

VIBRATION OF STRINGS AND OF AIR COLUMNS IN PIPES

WE must now proceed to apply the discussion of the foregoing chapter to some important practical cases. If we consider first the case of a stretched string or wire such as is used on any stringed instrument we find that waves will travel along it so rapidly that we shall be unable to follow them; but in all other respects the phenomenon is identical with that of the rope or rubber tube. We should therefore expect the direct and reflected wave systems to set up stationary vibration with the two fixed ends of the string always as nodes. The simplest way in which this can occur is when two consecutive nodes are at the fixed ends of the string and the intervening loop is at the middle. In this case the string vibrates as a whole, the centre swinging from side to side or up and down. It is also of course conceivable that alternate nodes might coincide in position with the ends of the string, the intervening node being at the centre. If this particular form of vibration could be induced we should have the string vibrating in two halves with a point of comparative rest at the centre. These and other possible modes of vibration may be studied by means of a sonometer—a wooden frame on which is stretched a string or wire. One end of the string is fixed to the frame, the other passes over a pulley and carries a scale pan in which weights may be placed. The weight placed in the pan together with the weight of the pan itself is a measure of the tension with which the string is being stretched. If this string be bowed in the usual way it will be found to emit a particular tone and to be vibrating as a whole. This latter fact can easily be verified by placing on the string a series of paper riders. All will be thrown into a state of commotion and probably all those at any distance from the ends will be thrown off the string altogether. On the other hand if the string be touched lightly at the centre with a camel's hair pencil or the corner of a handkerchief and bowed at about one quarter of its length from one end it will be found to emit a note an octave above the tone previously given. This time the paper riders will reveal the fact that the centre of the string is a point of minimum motion. The next possible method of vibration will have two nodes in the length of the string and will yield a note whose frequency is three times as great as that of the first note produced. A glance at Table III will show that this note must be an Octave and a Fifth, i.e. a Twelfth, above the first one. It can be induced by touching the string at a point one third of its length from either end, and bowing about the middle. The paper riders this time will show two nodes—one at the point touched and the other at the corresponding point, one third of the length of the string from the other end. These modes of vibration are illustrated in Fig. 13. Thus we find that the string is capable of vibrating in a great many different modes by dividing into different numbers of vibrating segments. It will be seen that whereas in the first mode the string is vibrating as a whole, in the second mode it is really vibrating as two strings, each of half the length, and in the third mode as three strings each of one third of the whole length of the string. From what follows it will be obvious that the frequencies of these modes are in the ratios 1 : 2 : 3 &c.

A theoretical investigation of the vibrations of a stretched string leads us to the following results.

(*a*) The frequency of the simplest mode of vibration of a stretched string is inversely proportional to the length of the string, so that if we halve the length

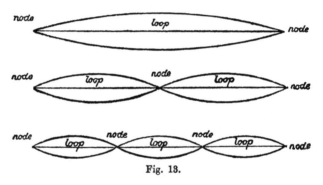

Fig. 13.

of a string, keeping its tension constant, we double its frequency of vibration and so raise its pitch an octave. This is easily verified by placing the movable bridge of the monochord under the mid-point of the string when either half of the string will be found to give the octave of the note given by the whole string.

(*b*) The frequency of vibration varies directly as

the square root of the stretching force. Thus in
order to raise by an octave the pitch of the note
given by the string the tension would require to be
increased four times. This relation can also be
verified by the sonometer although not quite so simply
as has just been suggested. Let weights be placed in
the scale pan until the note given by the string is the
same as that of a tuning-fork of convenient pitch—
say c. Weights are then added to the pan until the
note given by the string has risen to e. Now the
ratio of these two frequencies we know to be 5 : 4
and we should therefore expect the ratio of the
tensions to be 25 : 16—an expectation which will be
approximately realised.

(c) The frequency of vibration varies inversely as
the square root of the mass of unit length of the
string. Thus, if equal lengths of two wires of different
thicknesses be compared and one is found to weigh
four times as much as the other, and if these two
wires are stretched on a sonometer by the same
weights, the note given by the thinner will be found
to be an octave higher than that given by the thicker
one.

Let us now apply the discussion of stationary
vibration to the case of air in a pipe through which
two systems of waves are passing in opposite directions. Let Fig. 14a represent the displacements of the
layers of air in the pipe at a given instant and Fig. 14b

represent them when each of the constituent systems
has moved through half a wave-length (cf. Fig. 12).
Remembering the convention by the aid of which
those diagrams are made to represent vibrations in
air, we see that in the first figure all the layers of air
between A and C are displaced forwards (which we
shall take to be from left to right) while those between C and E are displaced backwards and those
between E and G forwards. In the second figure the
opposite is the case. Layers between A and C and

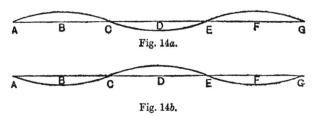

Fig. 14*a.*

Fig. 14*b.*

between E and G are displaced backwards while
those between C and E are displaced forwards. Thus
we see that the layers of air at B, D and F are loops,
i.e. have a maximum to-and-fro motion, while the
layers at A, C, E and G are nodes, i.e. have approximately no motion. We also see that at any instant
consecutive loops are displaced in opposite directions.
The flat top to the curve at B shows us that the
layers of air close to B are displaced by nearly the
same amount and we see that they are all displaced

in the same direction. This is true at both the
instants depicted and may be shown to be true for
intermediate instants also. It follows of course that
at a loop the layers of air maintain their relative
distances unchanged so that the pressure is normal.
If on the other hand we consider the layer represented by C, we notice that in the first figure the
layers of air immediately behind it are displaced
forwards while those immediately in front are displaced backwards. The layer at C will thus be
compressed by the layers on either side. In the
second figure the contrary is the case. Here the
layers of air immediately behind it are displaced
backwards while those immediately in front are displaced forwards. The layer at C is thus free to
expand in both directions and so becomes rarefied.
Thus the air at loops is continually in motion but
always remains at normal pressure, while the air at
nodes is at rest but is subject to periodic changes of
pressure.

Let us endeavour next to get a clear idea of how
air waves are reflected. If we consider a layer of
compressed air in the centre of a pipe we see at once
that if left to itself it would expand into the neighbouring layers on each side, compressing them, and
compressions would thus be propagated in both
directions. But we have already seen (p. 41) that
when air is transmitting a system of waves the layers

of air forming a compression are all moving forward.
This forward movement of the layers of air during
compression counteracts their tendency to expand
into the layers behind but encourages expansion
into the layers in front. For the same reason these
in turn expand into the layers in front of them and
thus the compression is propagated forwards only.
Now suppose the compression reaches the closed end
of the pipe. It is no longer able to expand into the
layers in front, and so, in order to relieve its pressure,
it must expand into the layers behind. These in
turn become compressed, and thus a compression is
propagated backwards, reflected from the closed end
of the pipe. Similar reasoning shows that when a
rarefaction reaches the closed end it is reflected
backwards as a rarefaction. Thus we have equal and
opposite systems of waves traversing the pipe, and so,
in the case of a closed pipe at least, we have all the
conditions necessary for setting up stationary vibrations. The air at the closed end will be unable to
move but will be able to sustain changes of pressure.
The air at the open end will be free to move but will
be unable to undergo changes of pressure. Thus the
open end of a pipe will be a loop and the closed end
a node. Using this condition we see that the following modes of vibration are possible for a closed organ
pipe. The simplest is shown in Fig. 15, both halves
of the vibration being represented. The air forming

the loop alternately moves in, compressing the air at
the closed end, and out, rarefying the air at the closed
end. Fig. 16 shows the next simplest method. Here
there is one node at the closed end and another at a
point one third of the length of the pipe from the
open end. Consideration of the figure will show that
in the first position the first mentioned of the two
nodes is a rarefaction due
to the motion away from
it of the air in the adjacent loop, while the second
node is a compression due
to the simultaneous mo-
tion towards it of the air
in both adjacent loops. In
the second position shown,
this state of affairs is re-
versed.

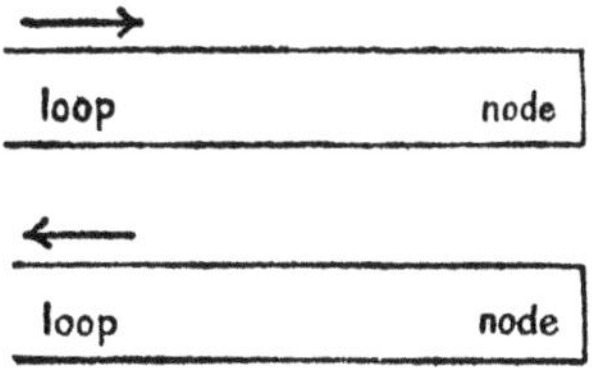

A little consideration
will show that in the next
possible mode of vibra-
tion the first node will be
one fifth of the length of the pipe from the open end,
the second three fifths from the open end and the third
at the closed end. Now the frequency of the note
given by a column of air in stationary vibration is, as
in the case of the string, found to be inversely proportional to its length if vibrating as a whole. The

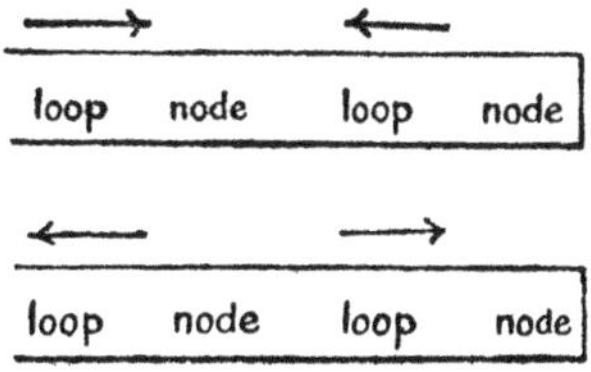

Fig. 15.

Fig. 16.

second mode of vibration is equivalent to three stopped pipes each one third of the length of the whole pipe and having their closed ends at the nodes and their open ends at the loops. The frequency of vibration in this case is therefore three times that corresponding to the first mode. Similarly for the third mode (which is equivalent to five stopped pipes each one fifth of the whole length of the pipe) the frequency is five times that of the first mode. The frequencies of the possible methods of vibrations are therefore in the ratio 1 : 3 : 5 &c.

This theory of the vibrations of air in a closed organ pipe is confirmed by a number of experiments. If for instance a closed pipe be overblown it jumps a twelfth, indicating a change from the first to the second mode of vibration. Also, if Koenig capsules (see page 12) be fitted to the pipe to be experimented on, much valuable information may be obtained. A capsule is fitted to an organ pipe by making the inside of the pipe act as the chamber which receives the air vibrations, the membrane being stretched over a hole bored in the side of the pipe at the point where the motion of the air is to be investigated. If the point is a node, changes of pressure will occur and the flame will show the jagged edge, while if the point is a loop, no changes of pressure will occur and the image of the flame will show a smooth edge. If for instance we take a closed pipe with Koenig capsules fitted at the two points of trisection and the flames be examined while the pipe is overblown, it will be found that the point nearer the open end is a node and that nearer the closed end a loop.

The case of the pipe open at both ends is some-what different. In this case when the compression whose progress we are considering reaches the open end of the pipe it is free to expand out into the open air surrounding the end. If the air had no inertia this expansion would only go on until the pressure of the air just outside and just inside were equal, after which there would be no further motion. Owing, however, to the inertia of the escaping air it tends to remain in motion when once started and so over-shoots the mark, leaving the air at the end of the pipe rarefied. This rarefaction is not filled up by the layers of air just outside the pipe as these are moving outwards. Therefore the layers of air behind it, just inside the tube, expand into it, and become them-selves rarefied in the process. Thus a rarefaction travels back along the pipe. In other words, when a compression comes to the open end of a pipe it is reflected as a rarefaction. Similar reasoning will show that a rarefaction is reflected as a compres-sion.

In the case of the open pipe it is obvious that we may have any mode of vibration consistent with the

two ends being loops. Thus the simplest mode will
be that in which the two ends are loops and the
centre is a node. In this case the air at the two ends
alternately moves in towards the centre and out from
the centre (see Fig. 17). The next simplest mode is
shown in Fig. 18. Here we have a loop at the middle
as well as the loops at the two ends, these loops being
separated by two nodes situated at points a quarter
of the length of the tube from each end. The next
mode is shown in Fig. 19, where we have again a node
at the centre, and the distance from loop to node all
along the tube is one-sixth of the whole length of the
tube.

Now when we come to compare the pitch of the
notes corresponding to the different modes of vibration of the open pipe with the pitch of those of a
closed pipe of the same length we notice one or two
interesting points of difference. In the first place we
notice that the simplest mode of vibration for the
open pipe is the same as for two closed pipes, each
half its length, with their closed ends together at the
centre of the pipe. After what has been already
said we should therefore expect that the note given
by the closed pipe when vibrating in its simplest
mode would be an Octave below that given by an
open pipe of the same length. That this is approximately true can easily be verified by blowing into an
open organ pipe and then closing the open end with

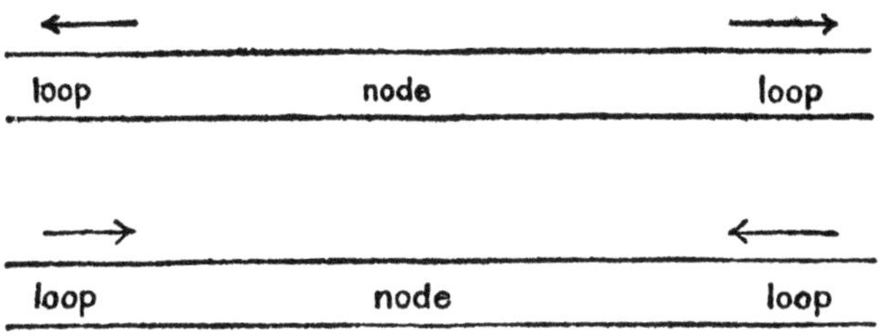

loop   node   loop

loop   node   loop

Fig. 17.

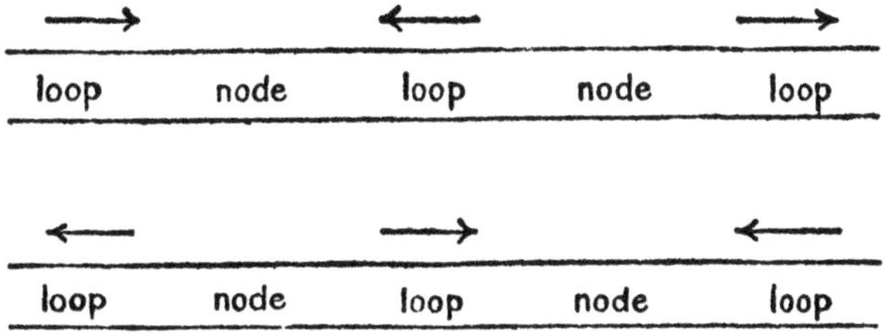

loop   node   loop   node   loop

loop   node   loop   node   loop

Fig. 18.

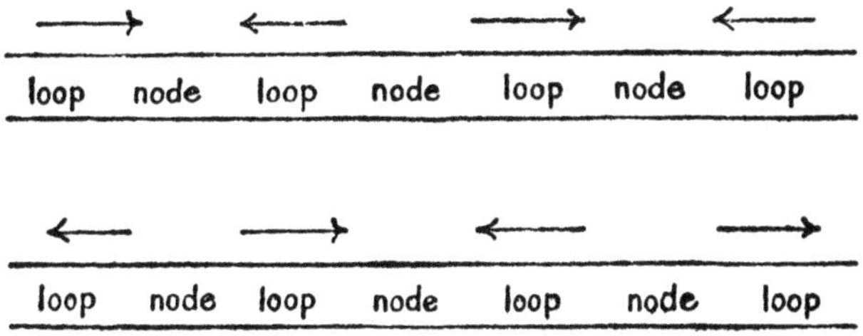

loop   node   loop   node   loop   node   loop

loop   node   loop   node   loop   node   loop

Fig. 19.

the hand. We shall find that the note drops nearly an Octave. Another interesting point of difference comes out when we compare the pitches of the various modes of vibration of the open pipe. The first mode is equivalent to two closed pipes each of half the length of the open pipe; the second is equivalent to four, each one quarter of the length; the third is equivalent to six, each one sixth of the length. It follows that the frequencies of the notes corresponding to these modes must be in the ratios 1 : 2 : 3, &c. It will be remembered that in the case of the closed pipe the corresponding ratios were 1 : 3 : 5, &c., and in the case of the vibrating string 1 : 2 : 3, &c. Now the series of notes whose frequencies are in the ratio 1 : 2 : 3, &c., are very important and will occupy a good deal of our attention later. Consideration of Table III will show that if C be taken as the first member of the series the next five will be c, g, c′, e′, g′. g is the Octave above G and so has a frequency $2 \times 3/2 = 3$. Similarly c′ is the Octave above c and so has a frequency $2 \times 2 = 4$. Next comes e′ which is two Octaves above E and so has a frequency $4 \times 5/4 = 5$. g′ is the Octave above g and so has a frequency $2 \times 3 = 6$. The next member of the harmonic series has a frequency 7, a frequency which we shall find is not represented on our scale. It lies between b′, which is the double Octave above B and so has a frequency $15/8 \times 4 = 7{\cdot}5$ and a′ which is the double Octave above A and so has a frequency $4 \times 5/3 = 6\cdot66$. The next two members of the series after g′ will be found to be c″, d″, and e″.

We may now sum up our discussion of the modes of vibrations of strings and pipes by saying that in all cases they are capable of vibrating in a great many different modes, but that whereas the strings and the open pipes can be made to give any note of the series whose frequencies are in the ratios 1 : 2 : 3, &c., the closed pipe can only give the odd members of this series.

CHAPTER V

RESONANCE—ANALYSIS OF VIBRATIONS— COMPLEXITY OF MUSICAL NOTES

In various places throughout the world there exist large masses of rock so delicately poised that they can be set rocking with comparatively little effort. A steady push produces practically no effect on them, but if a series of correctly timed pushes be given the stone begins to rock. It has a time of vibration of its own, and if the impulses given to it are timed so as to coincide with this natural period the energy communicated by each impulse goes to increase the amplitude of swing. The effect is

cumulative, but cannot be increased indefinitely.
Each oscillation of the rock dissipates energy—mainly
by friction on its support and friction against the surrounding air. It is this dissipation of energy which
causes it to come to rest again when it is set in
vibration and left to itself. The store of energy
which has been communicated to it is gradually
exhausted. Of course the greater the amplitude of
the swing the larger is the amount of energy dissipated
during that swing. Obviously then if each push we
give to the rock communicates to it a certain small
amount of energy, this amount will, to begin with,
exceed the amount dissipated in the course of the
swing. The swings will therefore increase in amplitude until exactly as much energy is dissipated in
the course of a swing as is received from the impulse.
When this point is reached the amplitude of swing
will remain constant.

Different vibrating systems vary very much in the
rate at which the energy of their swing is dissipated
and consequently in the rate at which their swings
"damp" or die out. In some cases the systems go
on swinging for a long time before coming to rest,
while in others they come to rest after one or two
oscillations. From what has been said it will be
clear that if anything is done to increase the rate
of damping of the vibrations of the rock the maximum amplitude which can be induced in it by

correctly timed impulses of given strength is thereby diminished. But the rate of damping has another very important bearing on this phenomenon of "resonance" as the response to timed impulses is called. If the rate of damping is very great, the effect of the first few impulses will soon have died out, so that the advantage of absolutely correct timing is in this case minimised. On the other hand if the rate of damping is very slow, the effect of the first few impulses persists for a long time, and if the timing of the impulses is not very accurate the later pulses will be more and more out of step with the earlier ones until they are actually opposing them instead of acting with them to produce a specially large effect. Thus, if the damping is very small, very correctly timed impulses will produce violent oscillation, but if the timing is not very accurate the oscillation produced is by comparison slight. On the other hand if the rate of damping is large the oscillation produced by timed impulses is, by comparison with the former case, small, and if the timing is not quite accurate no very marked difference in the amplitude of oscillation is produced.

Let us now pass to acoustical illustrations of these facts. It is of course from these that the term resonance has come to be applied to the whole phenomenon. Suppose we take a stout tuning-fork whose frequency of vibration is 256. The prongs are of steel and it requires very considerable effort on our part to produce in them any appreciable displacement. That these prongs should be capable of being set in vibration by pulses of air seems even less credible than that a mass of rock weighing say 60 tons (the supposed weight of the Logan stone at Land's End) can be set in motion by a series of pushes given by the hand. Yet, if we take another fork of identically the same frequency and make it sound strongly in the neighbourhood of the first, we shall find that when this second fork is removed the first one is sounding. A single pulse of air is a feeble thing, but the fork has been receiving a series of these pulses accurately timed at the rate of 256 per second, and although the contribution of each may be infinitesimal their combined effect is very marked. Now repeat the experiment, but this time after loading one of the forks with a small pellet of wax. The pellet may be so small that when the two forks are sounded together only about 2 beats per second are heard. That will mean that the loaded fork has now a frequency of about 254. When this has been done the phenomenon of resonance will be found to have disappeared almost entirely. The tuning-fork is a case of a vibrating system in which the damping is very slight—hence the marked response to the accurately tuned fork and the failure to respond appreciably for very slight mistuning.

Next let us take an empty bottle and blow across the neck of it. A definite musical note will result—not perhaps very clear, but unmistakable in pitch. This note can be tuned to some extent. Its pitch will be raised by partially filling the bottle with water and lowered by partially shading the opening of the neck with a card. The bottle can thus be brought into unison with a tuning-fork—let us say a fork giving 512 vibrations per second. If now the fork is held over the open neck of the bottle the impulses arriving from the fork will set the air contained in the bottle into vibration, and the sound of the fork will be reinforced. If the fork be so loaded with wax as to alter its frequency by 12 and so reduce it to 500, the bottle will still reinforce the note and almost as strongly as before. Indeed if a fork differing in pitch from the former by a semitone (i.e. having a frequency of about 480) be held over the mouth of the bottle, the resonance will still be quite perceptible although distinctly more feeble. The explanation of these facts is that the air in the bottle is a system for which the rate of damping is very great indeed. The vibrations can be evoked by blowing, as has been indicated, but immediately the blast of air is stopped the vibrations die out and no sound can be heard. This rapid damping explains why the system should respond, with hardly diminished intensity, to impulses not accurately timed to its own period—i.e. to notes of sensibly different pitch.

An intermediate case is that of the stretched string. Here the damping is as a rule greater than for a tuning-fork but much less than for a volume of air. What may be called the sharpness of resonance is therefore in this case less than that of the tuning-fork but greater than the air column.

We next pass to consider a mathematical theorem published by Fourier in 1822 and known as Fourier's Theorem. Its connection with what has gone before will not at first be apparent but will become clear later. The theorem states that any periodic vibration however complex may be considered as built up of a series of simple harmonic vibrations (the type given by a pendulum bob) whose frequencies are in the ratios $1 : 2 : 3 : 4$ &c., the frequency of the complex vibration itself being the first member of the series. This series is called the harmonic series. The statement is at first sight a very surprising one. It means that any displacement diagram, however complicated, can, by the use of the method used on page 38, be built up out of a series of the smooth simple harmonic displacement diagrams to which attention has already been drawn (page 31), even when we confine ourselves to choosing such of these as have frequencies in the ratio of the whole numbers and no others. When we reflect that if this is true it must apply also to the straight line displacement diagram of Fig. 6, it seems almost incredible that it should be capable of synthesis from a series of simple harmonic curves. Of course we have an infinite series of these smooth curves at our disposal and we can adjust their relative amplitudes and relative phases (relative positions along the axis) as we please, but the theoretical discussion of the theorem shows that the synthesis can only be effected in one way. If we are given a complex displacement diagram and are required to select from the harmonic series a certain number of components such that their displacement diagrams when compounded will give the complex one, we shall find that the problem has only one solution. There is only one selection which will satisfy the requirement, and this selection will only satisfy it for one particular amplitude of each component and one particular position of the component on the axis relative to the others. Looking at the matter from the point of view of analysis we may say that if we are given the complicated vibration referred to and asked to analyse it into terms of the harmonic series, the analysis can be effected in only one way—the particular members of the series which are present, their relative amplitudes and relative phases are all completely determined.

Of course this is not the only possible method of analysing a complex vibration. We need not confine

ourselves to harmonic components, and it is evident
that if we do not do so it would be easy to draw
two or more displacement diagrams whose ordinates
would when added or subtracted give us the complex
curve required. It therefore becomes important for
us to consider whether analysis in terms of harmonic
components has any particular advantages for us over
other possible methods. The first important fact
from this point of view is that harmonic analysis can
be carried out practically by means of the phenomenon
of resonance already discussed. If the complex
vibration of a system A be communicated to another
system B, this second system will be set in resonant
vibration if, on analysis of the vibration of A, it
appears that a simple harmonic component of the
period of the vibration of B is present. This cannot
be predicted of any other method of analysis. The
second important consideration is that this particular
method of analysis is almost certainly the one adopted
by the ear, which is a practical harmonic analyser.
This law of the action of the ear was stated by
G. S. Ohm and may be expressed as follows: the
ear only experiences the sensation of a simple tone
when it is excited by a simple harmonic vibration.
It analyses every other periodic vibration into a
series of simple harmonic vibrations (the members of
Fourier's series) each corresponding to the sensation
of a simple tone.

That the air, like other media, is capable of transmitting simultaneously several sets of waves, is obvious from our common experience. In a room in which several people are talking at once, the sounds made by the individual voices all reach the ear through the same air and we can, by an act of attention, separate from the combined noise the voice of any one individual and listen only to that. As a rule we hear best the conversation of those in our immediate neighbourhood, but it is often surprising how difficult it is to hear what our neighbour is saying if a conversation in which we are interested is being carried on in a more distant part of the room, and our attention becomes focussed on that. Again in following a vocal or instrumental quartette we can concentrate our attention on any one part and follow that. This brings us face to face with a very wonderful property of the ear—its power of analysing complex sounds. Remember that the membrane of the ear can only have one motion at any particular instant. It goes through a series of displacements which is the resultant of all those due to the several wave systems, and in this resultant the ear is able to detect and isolate the components. This far surpasses any power of analysis which the eye possesses. Yet even here we have not by any means reached the limit of the power of analysis of the ear. When we listen to a musical note played on the piano or sung by the voice, we are not, as a rule, conscious that the sensation is an extremely complex one. When we first meet the statement that a single note heard under these circumstances is not a single note at all but a whole series of single notes, we do so with surprise. Nevertheless such is indeed the case and with a little assistance and practice the ear will carry out this analysis too. We find that in almost every case there is associated with what is apparently a single note a whole series of others forming with it the harmonic series and having frequencies bearing to the frequency of the note itself the ratios 2, 3, 4, 5 &c. to 1. The fact that these partial tones, as we shall call the associated tones, usually escape observation is not difficult to explain. In separating sounds coming from different sources the ear may be assisted by many small differences. The sounds probably start differently, they may differ in duration, in the certainty with which they can be sustained, and in the manner in which they start and die away. On the other hand in analysing a complex note into its constituents these aids are not, as a rule, available. Then again the separation of sounds coming from different sources is often of the greatest service to us and so is habitually practised while the analysis of a note into its elements can rarely fulfil any useful purpose.

Nevertheless these partial tones are of the very

greatest importance in music and the fact that few people have cultivated the art of detecting them in no way affects their importance. Their presence in the case of notes sounded on the piano may be readily demonstrated. Depress the key c′ (see Table I) without causing it to sound. This will raise the damper from the string and so leave it free to vibrate. Next sound the note c strongly, if necessary striking it several times in succession. If there is, associated with the note c, a partial tone of frequency c′ then the string corresponding to this will be set in vibration by resonance and when the key corresponding to c has been released c′ will be heard sounding if its key is still kept down. The same experiment ought to be repeated with b and d′ instead of c′ so that it may be clear that the phenomenon is only exhibited by certain particular notes—those in fact which form with c the harmonic series already alluded to. The experiment will succeed with g′ and with c″ without any trouble but the higher members of the series—e″, g″, and c″ are a little hard to detect. A method which Helmholtz used to detect these partial tones was to have small hollow brass air chambers with two apertures one of which was fitted into the ear while the other was directed towards the source of sound. The shape and size of these resonators could be adjusted to tune them so that the contained air would resound to a note of any required pitch.

When placed to the ear they reinforced their own particular tone if it was sounded, even if it were only a partial tone in a more complex note. By the use of these resonators Helmholtz showed the existence of partial tones in notes produced by strings and other musical instruments.

Perhaps however the most satisfactory and convincing demonstration of all is the perception of these partial tones by the unaided ear. This is merely a matter of attention and practice. If the note, corresponding in pitch to the partial which it is desired to hear, be first sounded very gently as a guide to the ear and the note of which it is a partial be then strongly sounded, the ear will, after a time, have little difficulty in recognising the musical note as a complex and picking out its more important constituent partial tones. In the case of the human voice, which is particularly rich in partials, some ten or twelve of these have been detected.

We are now in a position to realise fully how wonderful the power of analysis possessed by the ear really is. From the complex periodic motion of the air in the ear passage—a motion which may be the resultant of some eight or ten separate components the ear is able to perceive separately each of the components.

Thus we have strong evidence for the belief that sounding bodies such as stretched strings and columns of air are not only capable of being made to vibrate successively in a series of modes giving a series of different notes but that as ordinarily excited they give simultaneously a number of different notes. The corresponding methods of vibration coexist and the displacements of the various parts of the vibrating body are, at any instant, the resultant of the displacements which it would have had due to the separate component vibrations. Hereafter we shall use the term note to mean the complex musical sounds of definite pitch produced by musical instruments and by the voice. The simple unanalysable tones of which these are composed we shall call partials. The lowest member of the harmonic series—the one which gives the pitch to the note—we shall call the prime, or first partial. The others will be the second, third &c. partials.

We have already connected quality with displacement diagrams. It is now easy to see that the number and relative intensities of the partials present in a given note will determine the character of the displacement diagram and so the quality of the note which it represents. We shall proceed to consider arguments which lend further support to the conclusion that a sounding body vibrates simultaneously in a number of its modes, giving in consequence a series of simple tones, and that the presence and relative intensities of these partial tones give the

note in question its distinctive quality. Tones which
are brilliant or even harsh in quality we shall find
to be rich in partials, while tones which are soft or
even dull are those in which the higher partials are
feeble or absent. As examples of the first may be
instanced strings struck or plucked with hard instruments, while as examples of the latter we may take
the tuning-fork and the closed, or stopped, organ
pipe. The stretched string or wire of a sonometer
is very convenient for experiments on the relation
of partial tones to quality. Let the string be plucked
or bowed somewhere near one end, and while it is
sounding let its middle point be lightly damped
with a feather or the corner of a handkerchief. The
mid-point of the string will be brought to rest, and
as the first mode of vibration requires this point to
be in motion (see Fig. 13), the prime tone will disappear and we shall hear clearly what the prominence
of this tone was masking, the second partial whose
pitch is an octave above the pitch of the prime.
Now merely damping the centre of the string could
not bring into existence a mode of vibration not
previously present and so we are forced to conclude
that the second mode of vibration of the string must
have been coexisting with the first. In the same
way we can obtain the third partial. If the string
be once more plucked or bowed near one end, and
this time be damped at a point one third of its length

from either end, the Twelfth of the normal pitch of the string will be heard sounding strongly. This is due to the fact that both the prime and second partials require the point of trisection of the string to be in motion, and so damping this point stops both these modes of vibration and gives in consequence a new prominence to the third partial. This partial also must have been a constituent tone of the original note given by the wire. The process can of course be extended to higher partials in a similar way, and in order to make the proof of the existence of these partials in the note given by the string quite convincing, it is well in each case, after obtaining a particular partial by damping, to pluck or bow the string again and listen for that partial in the resulting note. In the case of the first few members of the series there will be no difficulty in isolating it by an act of attention, and the demonstration of its presence will be complete.

So far we have always excited the string at a point near one end and have found all the lower partials quite prominent. Now let us examine the effect of bowing or plucking at the centre. We shall find at once a marked difference in quality. The quality of the note given when the centre of the string is attacked is dull and nasal, the quality when the point of attack is moved to the end tends to be harsh and tinkling. A moment's consideration will convince us that the second, fourth, sixth &c. modes of vibration of the string require a node at the centre. If then we bow or pluck the string at the centre all the even partials must be absent. If on the other hand we excite a point on the string one tenth of its length from either end, the lowest partial which requires a node there is the tenth and the next lowest is the twentieth, so that the full series of partials below the tenth may be present and those are the only ones of any practical importance. In an exactly similar way the upper partials may be called in to explain the very marked difference in quality between a stopped and an open organ pipe of the same pitch. We have already seen in Chapter IV that the open organ pipe is capable of vibrating so as to give any note of the harmonic series while the closed organ pipe can only give the odd members of that series. It follows that the quality of the former should be brighter than that of the latter, and this we find to be the case.

It is perhaps well to mention at this point that all partials are not harmonic—that is to say there are some vibrating bodies whose different modes of vibration have frequencies the ratios of which to the frequency of the prime cannot be represented by whole numbers. As a rule these have no very important musical application although inharmonic partials are prominent in bells, cymbals and instruments of the kind. In the case of wide organ pipes the discussion given in Chapter IV is only approximate and the possible modes of vibration are not strictly harmonics of the prime. The intensity of the corresponding partials is on this account much more feeble than would otherwise be the case.

CHAPTER VI

STRUCTURE AND ACTION OF THE EAR

In a volume of the present size and scope any detailed treatment of the structure and action of the ear would be quite out of place, but the phenomena with which we have been dealing make it possible for us to propose at this point a mechanical theory of the action of the ear which will be of the greatest service to us in what follows, and which has considerable experimental support. Let us first of all consider the behaviour of a mechanical model whose structure is suggested by the structure of the ear. Suppose we have a long conical box filled with liquid and divided longitudinally into three tapering compartments so that its cross-section resembles Fig. 20. AB is a membrane, while the partition AC consists of a series of stretched strings connected together by a membrane, so that any motion of the

fluid may the more easily be communicated to them.
The base and sides of the cone are rigid, but the

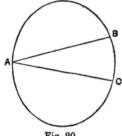

Fig. 20.

former contains two apertures
one of which gives access to
the uppermost chamber while
the other gives access to the
lowest. These apertures are
closed with membranes. There
is a small passage at the vertex of the cone which connects
the uppermost and lowest compartments. If now the mem-
brane giving access to the uppermost compartment be
caused to vibrate, its vibrations will be transmitted
through the fluid to the vertex of the cone, through
the small passage into the lowest compartment, and
so down to the membrane closing this compartment.
At the same time they will be transmitted through the
membranous partitions separating the three compartments. Each time the membranous window giving
access to the upper compartment is driven in, the
corresponding window of the lowest compartment
will be driven out, and vice versa. The effect of
this transmission of vibrations will be to set the
fluid in the middle compartment vibrating also,
the vibrations being transmitted to it through the
membranous walls. Let us suppose further that
the strings which form the texture of the lower wall

of the middle compartment form a series, the length and tension of which are so adjusted that their frequencies of vibration diminish gradually from the vertex to the base of the cone and that the damping of the vibrations of these strings is appreciable. If a simple harmonic vibration be now imposed on the upper membranous window the resulting vibrations will pass through the fluids inside, will act on the strings and those strings which are nearest the frequency of the imposed vibration will be set vibrating by resonance, while the others will remain practically at rest. Let us see now how far this model would show the properties which we know the ear actually to possess.

It could perceive loudness. The louder the sound the greater would be the amplitude of vibration of the window, the greater the amplitude of the fluid motion and therefore the greater the amplitude of the strings affected.

It could perceive pitch. High notes would affect the short tightly stretched strings. Low notes would affect the longer strings. From the particular members of the series of strings which were affected we could deduce the pitch of the exciting sound.

It could effect the analysis of complex notes. Each partial tone present in the note would affect its own particular group of strings. From the groups of strings affected and their relative amplitudes we

could at once tell the pitch of the partials which
were present and their relative intensities. This is
a consideration of the utmost importance. It is
almost impossible to conceive any other mechanism
whereby this extraordinary property of the human
ear could be imitated. A very good example of the
process here suggested is given if we press down the
loud pedal of a piano so as to remove the dampers
from the strings and then sing or whistle into it a
note of any pitch. The piano will effect an analysis,
each string of the piano which corresponds in pitch
to one of the harmonic partials of the note being set
in resonant vibration, and the instrument will give
back a note not only of the same pitch but also in
point of quality quite a good imitation of the original
note.

The model would also explain very simply the
obvious if indefinable relationship which we perceive
between the sensations produced by certain pairs of
notes when sounded successively—for example two
notes giving the interval of an Octave. Let us
suppose we sound a note whose pitch is c. If this
note is sounded on an instrument which gives the
associated partials we shall have sounding at the same
time c′, g′, c″, e″, and g″. Now suppose the Octave
above this note to be sounded—also with its series of
partials. This will give us c′ as the prime tone and
c″, g″, &c., as the partial tones. It will be noticed

that the second note merely emphasises tones which were present before and adds nothing new of its own. The second note only affects groups of strings which were already in action. In this way the relationship of these two notes is easily explained and the explanation will be found to hold for all the simple intervals. If we take for instance the interval of the Fifth—next to the Octave the closest and most obvious relationship between pairs of notes—it will readily be seen that a similar explanation suggests itself. The lower note c carries with it as before c', g', c'', e'', g'', &c. The upper note g carries with it g', d'', g'', &c. Here it will be observed that the upper note does contribute something new—it does affect groups of strings not affected by the stimulus of the lower note—but at the same time the two notes have several common partials, every third partial of the lower note coinciding in pitch with every second partial of the upper note, and this common content is quite sufficient to explain the relationship. This view is further strengthened by the discovery that those intervals for which the relationship of the notes seems to our ears to be most distant are exactly those for which the common content is very small.

Finally our model explains the phenomenon of beats. If two notes are sufficiently close in pitch to act on the same strings, then those strings which are

subject to the joint action of the two notes will
have a variable amplitude of vibration which will go
through a series of maxima and minima, the number

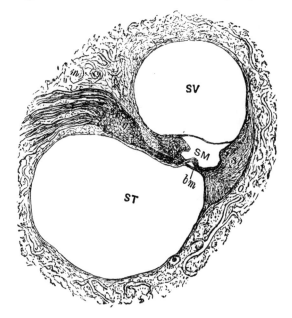

Fig. 21.

of complete cycles so executed in one second being
equal to their difference in frequency.

Now the mechanical model which we have taken

as the basis of the foregoing discussion approximately reproduces the actual structure of the inner ear (see Fig. 21). Here we have our tapering cavity filled with fluid but coiled into the form of a snail-shell and so known as the *cochlea*. It is completely surrounded by a hard bony wall except for two small openings at the base. One of these, the upper, is a small oval aperture called the *fenestra ovalis*; the lower is a small round aperture called the *fenestra rotunda*. Both are closed by membranes. The interior of the cochlea is divided like our model into three compartments by longitudinal membranous partitions. The uppermost of these is the *scala vestibuli SV*, the lowest is the *scala tympani ST* while the middle one is the *scala media SM*. The membrane separating the scala media from the scala tympani is called the *basilar membrane bm* and has a structure consisting of stretched transverse fibres. The tension of the membrane in the direction of these fibres being considerably greater than its tension at right angles to them the effect is practically the same as if they were a series of stretched strings connected by the membrane. This membrane carries the nerve endings. The fenestra ovalis is connected by a chain of small bones with the *membrana tympani* or drum of the ear. These bones lie in a cavity called the middle ear in which the pressure of the air is kept normal since the cavity connects with the outer air through the

Eustachian tube which is periodically opened in the act of swallowing. The vibrations of the air pass into the outer ear and act on the membrana tympani. This takes up the vibrations and transmits them by means of the chain of small bones to the fenestra ovalis. The facility with which the membrana tympani takes up these vibrations is very much reduced if the pressure of the air in the middle ear becomes large. Accidentally this sometimes happens and temporary deafness ensues until the act of swallowing opens the Eustachian tube and reduces the pressure to normal, when the deafness disappears. The chain of small bones acts like a compound lever, reducing the amplitude of the vibrations in the ratio of 3 : 2, increasing their force in the inverse ratio and concentrating it on the much smaller area of the fenestra ovalis. Arrived at this oval window the vibrations pass up the scala vestibuli, through a little passage at the vertex—*the heliocotrema*—and then travel down the scala tympani to the round window. According to our theory these vibrations set certain of the fibres of the basilar membrane into resonant vibration and so stimulate the corresponding nerve endings. The analogy with our model is practically complete.

Now before we rest satisfied with this view of the process of hearing it will be well to consider what objections may be urged to it and how far we can get any confirmatory evidence. It will be obvious at once that if there is comparatively little damping one serious objection would have to be met. In this case each fibre of the basilar membrane would respond appreciably to its own particular note and to no others. Therefore if a sound were made, and the pitch gradually raised we should expect our sensation to be discontinuous. On the other hand if there is a reasonable amount of damping this objection disappears. The note will affect, not one fibre but a group of fibres, and as the pitch is gradually raised there will be no discontinuity in the sensation—the fibres constituting the group change progressively, shorter ones being taken in to the group and longer ones being rejected as the pitch of the exciting note rises. This question of damping is an important one and a certain amount of information about it may be obtained by a study of rapid trills. It is a well-known fact that very rapid trills become confused and indistinct. This indistinctness does not depend on the instrument on which they are executed and so must depend on the ear itself. The existence of this confusion in the case of rapid trills is almost enough in itself to establish the fact that the ear contains a number of separate vibrating parts. In order that a single vibrating body should respond to a series of vibrations corresponding to the range of hearing, the damping of its vibrations would have to be practically infinite and trills would be distinct no matter what their rapidity of execution might be. Another fact of importance emerges in this connection and strengthens our argument considerably. The rapidity for which a trill remains distinct depends on the pitch of the note upon which it is executed. Rapid trills in the treble are quite as distinct as much slower ones in the bass. Now this is just what we should expect. Suppose the damping for all the fibres is such that the amplitude falls to a tenth of its value in 30 vibrations. The time occupied by these vibrations will be much less for notes of high than for notes of low pitch. Thus C, frequency 128, would fall to one tenth of its amplitude in 30/128 seconds or about one quarter of a second, while c″, frequency 1024, falls to one tenth of its original amplitude in 30/1024 or less than the thirtieth of a second. So far then our theory is in accord with the facts. It is of course impossible to make any exact measurements of the damping but it is quite possible to get an approximate value for it. Thus, following Helmholtz, we may start from the fact that a trill of 10 notes per second executed on A, frequency 110, is distinct. In this case each note is struck five times per second. The trill could only be distinct if in the interval of a fifth of a second the amplitude of vibration fell to about one tenth of its original value. But one fifth of a second is the time occupied by 22 complete vibrations. We take therefore as a rough estimate of the rate of damping that in which the amplitude falls to one tenth of its value in the course of 22 vibrations. Now from this fact theory enables us to deduce something about the range of tones to which a fibre will give appreciable response. We find for instance, that with this rate of damping the fibre ought to respond to vibrations differing from its own proper tone by a quarter of a tone with an intensity equal to one tenth of the intensity with which it would respond to a tone of exactly its own frequency. Now shakes executed on notes much lower than A soon become indistinct if performed at the speed suggested, so that no great error will be introduced if we assume the range of tones to which any individual fibre will respond to include those lying within the limits of a semitone either above or below its own proper tone.

There is another line of evidence which brings us to much the same conclusion. We have already touched on the question of beats and reference has been made to the fact that beats can only occur when the two sets of vibrations act together on the same vibrating system. This system must also have direct connexion with the nerves and so must, on our hypothesis, be one fibre or a group of fibres of the basilar membrane. It is clear then, that if two notes be separated by an interval greater than about a tone, no beats can be heard as the two groups affected will cease to have any fibres in common. Let it be clearly borne in mind that in what follows we are dealing with pure tones—i.e. tones free from any associated partials. If two pure tones of the same frequency are sounded together strongly, and the frequency of one of them be then slowly raised, we at once hear beats—slow at first but becoming more and more rapid. To begin with, the ear hears them separately, but as their rapidity increases we hear, in place of the separate beats, a kind of continuous roughness. This roughness becomes more and more harsh and unpleasant until a maximum of harshness seems to be attained after which the roughness diminishes and finally disappears. There can be very little doubt that the cause of the roughness is rapid beating. Intermittent sensations are usually unpleasant, as in the case of a flickering candle, and when we watch a stretched wire beating under the joint action of two forks of nearly equal frequency it is difficult to resist the conclusion that if the action on our nerve endings at all resembles it the sensation ought to be a very unpleasant one indeed. The gradual dis-appearance of the harsh character of the sensation may be due to one of two causes—or perhaps to both together. It may be due merely to the increased rapidity of the beats producing in the end a sensation which is practically continuous. In the neighbourhood of c, frequency 512, the harshness seems to be a maximum when the number of beats per second is about 32. On the other hand for C, frequency 64, the interval of the Fifth gives $3/2 \times 64 = 96$. If these two notes be sounded together we have a frequency difference of 32, and yet if the tones are pure there is no trace of harshness. Obviously then the rapidity of the beats is not the only factor. The other possible cause is the increased interval between the two beating notes and it is sufficient to point out here that according to our deduction two notes must be separated by an interval not much greater than a tone if the two groups of resonators which they affect are to have any fibres in common. It is hardly too much to claim that this will be found to hold for pure tones with certain exceptions to be afterwards dealt with. A study of the beating of pure tones then corroborates our hypothesis as to the action of the ear. The theory may be summed up in the following sentences due to Professor McKendrick.

(1) In the cochlea there are vibrators tuned to frequencies within the limits of hearing, say from 30 to 40,000 or 50,000 vibrations per second.

(2) Each vibrator is capable of exciting its appropriate nerve filament or filaments, so that a nervous impulse, corresponding to the frequency of the vibrator, is transmitted to the brain—not corresponding necessarily, as regards the number of nervous

impulses, but in such a way that when the impulses along a particular nerve filament reach the brain, a state of consciousness is aroused which does correspond with the number of the physical stimuli and with the period of the auditory vibrator.

(3) The mass of each vibrator is such that it will be easily set in motion, and after the stimulus has ceased, it will readily come to rest.

(4) Damping arrangements exist in the ear so as to extinguish quickly movements of the vibrators.

(5) If a simple tone falls on the ear, there is a particular movement of the base of the stapes (the small bone attached to the oval window) which will affect all the parts, causing them to move; but any part whose natural period is nearly the same as that of the sound will respond on the principle of sympathetic resonance, a particular nerve filament or filaments will be affected, and a sensation of a tone of definite pitch will be experienced, thus accounting for discrimination in pitch.

(6) Intensity or loudness will depend on the amplitude of movement of the vibrating body, and consequently on the intensity of nerve stimulation.

(7) If a compound wave of pressure be communicated by the base of the stapes, it will be resolved into its constituents by the vibrators corresponding to the tones existing in it, each picking out its appropriate portion of the wave, and thus irritating

corresponding nerve filaments. In this manner nervous impulses are transmitted to the brain, where they are fused in such a way as to give rise to a sensation of a particular quality or character, but still so imperfectly fused, that each constituent, by a strong effort of attention, may be separately recognised.

CHAPTER VII

CONSONANT INTERVALS

In the last chapter it was suggested that dissonance is to be explained by the rapid beating of the two notes forming the dissonant interval. This explanation can of course only apply to the cases of dissonance between notes lying within the interval of a Minor Third. On the other hand, we know that some of the intervals greater than a Minor Third are extremely dissonant, the Seventh being one of the most dissonant of all. The difficulty here disappears when we remember the existence of partial tones. In the case of the Octave we remember that every second partial of the lower note coincides with a partial of the upper note, thus we have a long series of coincident partials of diminishing importance.   If

now the upper note of the interval is lowered a
semitone in pitch, we shall have the interval of the
Seventh, and at the same time each partial of the
upper note, which previously coincided with a partial
of the lower note, will now be a semitone out of tune
with it and so will give rapid beats and dissonance.
In support of this view it may be stated that where
the intervals are simple tones, free from associated
partials, the dissonance of the Seventh almost disappears, although it strikes us as a somewhat unusual
interval.   One reason why the dissonance does not
altogether disappear will be discussed later under
combination tones.   Thus we see that in order to
determine theoretically whether or no an interval
is consonant, we must consider not only whether
beats may occur between the two primes themselves,
but also whether beats may occur between higher
partials.   In estimating the dissonance of particular
intervals, we shall assume first of all that each note
carries with it the first six partials, and that their
importance diminishes as their order increases.   Thus,
other things being equal, an interval in which the two
primes are within the beating distance will be more
dissonant than an interval where the beating is due
to one prime and the second partial of the other,
while this in turn will be more dissonant than an
interval where the beating occurs between two upper
partials.

Let us first of all apply these principles to the discussion of the octave. Here we have a case of absolute consonance. Every partial of the upper note coincides with one of the partials of the lower. Also the interval is very sharply bounded by dissonance on either side because of the fact that any mistuning of either note throws out of tune each pair of coincident partials. The prime of the upper note coincides with the second partial of the lower if the interval is correctly tuned, and it is here that any error of tuning reveals itself most clearly. The mistuning of the interval gives rise to slow beats between those two tones which, by a proper fixing of the attention, it is quite possible to count and to distinguish from the beats of higher partials. This may be illustrated by an experiment carried out with a modification of Dove's siren due to Helmholtz. In this form there are two perforated wind-chests and two perforated disks. The two disks rotate together, being fixed to the same spindle. The lower wind-chest is fixed while the other can be rotated. Each wind-chest and disk is perforated with four rows of holes, the rows in the lower chest and disk containing as a rule 8, 10, 12 and 18 holes respectively, while those in the upper chest and disk contain 9, 12, 15 and 16 holes. Any one or more of these rows can be brought into action at a time. If now the 8-hole row is opened in the lower chest and the 16-hole row

in the upper, then at whatever speed the spindle may
be driven the resulting interval is always a perfect
Octave—there is absolute consonance and no trace
of beats. If now the upper wind-chest is made to
revolve, the frequency of the air-puffs coming from it
will be altered. If it rotates in the same direction
as its perforated disk the frequency of the puffs will
be diminished, if in the opposite direction the frequency of the puffs will be increased. In either case
the consonance will be disturbed and beats will be
heard.

What has been said of the Octave applies almost
without modification to the Twelfth. Here the first
coincidence, and therefore the one on which the
definition of the interval mainly depends, is that
between the upper prime and the third partial of
the lower while the other partials of the upper note
coincide with every third partial of the lower. Like
the Octave it is an absolute consonance but less
clearly defined, as an interval, because of the relatively weaker beats between the prime and the
third partial. Following out this line of investigation
we shall find that absolute consonances occur only
for pairs of notes such that the prime of the one
coincides with a partial of the other, and as the next
of the series is the double Octave it is obvious that
the remaining absolute consonances are of comparatively little importance.

We come next to the consideration of intervals
defined by the coincidence of two partials, one belonging to each note of the combination. Taking the
interval of the Fifth and assuming the frequencies of
the two notes forming the interval to be 300 and 200,
we see that we get the following series of frequencies
for the partials:

	300		600		900		1200
200		400	600	800		1000	1200

Here the second partial of the higher note coincides
with the third of the lower. It will be readily seen
that the orders of the two partials, whose coincidence defines the interval, give the ratio of the
frequencies of the two notes forming the interval.
In this case it is the second partial of one note and
the third of the other which define the interval,
and the ratio of the frequencies is 2 : 3. This is
true for all intervals. In the case of the Fourth,
for instance, where we have already seen that the
ratio of the frequencies is 3 : 4, we shall find that
the interval is defined by the coincidence of the
fourth partial of the one note with the third of
the other. Bearing this rule in mind we shall see
that all important intervals are, as we should expect, defined by the coincidence of comparatively
low partials.

Interval	Ratio of Frequencies	Partial of Upper Note	Partial of Lower Note
Unison ...	1 : 1	First	First
Octave ...	2 : 1	First	Second
Twelfth ...	3 : 1	First	Third
Double Octave	4 : 1	First	Fourth
Fifth ...	3 : 2	Second	Third
Tenth ...	5 : 2	Second	Fifth
Fourth ...	4 : 3	Third	Fourth
Major Sixth	5 : 3	Third	Fifth
Major Third	5 : 4	Fourth	Fifth
Minor Third	6 : 5	Fifth	Sixth
Minor Sixth	8 : 5	Fifth	Eighth

Let us next examine the effect on the pairs of coincident partials of errors in the tuning of the notes. Take first a mistuned Octave in which the frequencies of the notes are 200 and 101. The second partial of the lower note will have a frequency 202, and we shall hear two beats per second between it and the upper note, frequency 200. On the other hand if the upper note is mistuned by 1, we shall have the interval 201 : 100. In this case the second partial of the lower note is 200, and we shall only have one beat per second between it and the upper note. Thus the number of beats per second is 1 or 2 if the frequency of one of the notes be inaccurate by 1 vibration per second, according as the inaccuracy is in the upper or the lower note. Take next the mistuned fifth 201 : 300. The third partial of the lower note is 603, the second partial of the upper is 600, and between these two we have 3 beats per second. If the fifth is 200 : 301, the two partials which ought to coincide have frequencies 600 and 602, and the number of beats is 2. This indicates a general rule which will be found to hold for all intervals. If one of the two notes forming the interval is mistuned by one vibration per second, then the two numbers defining the frequency ratio give respectively the number of beats between the two partials defining the interval, according as it is the higher or the lower note which is mistuned. Mistuning the lower note gives the larger number of beats per second.

From these facts it is evident that the higher the orders of the two partials whose coincidence defines the interval, the more accurate must the tuning be if disagreeable beating is to be avoided. At the same time, it must not be forgotten that where the partials in question are high, the beats will be much less prominent, partly on account of the weakness of the high partials which cause the beats, and partly because, as we shall see, there is generally some roughness present in these consonances due to the beating of lower and more prominent partials. Also for these intervals it is less true than for those defined by lower pairs of partials that neighbouring intervals must be dissonant. Very slight inaccuracy in tuning causes fairly rapid beating in the case of the Minor Third and Minor Sixth, and so a change of a

semitone in one of the notes forming either of these
intervals may well cause such rapid beating that
the resulting roughness is hardly noticeable. But
for the most part it may be taken as a guiding
principle in any discussion of the relative consonance
of various intervals that those close to an absolute
consonance or to one defined by low partials must be
dissonant, and that the more consonant an interval is
the more dissonant must its neighbours be.

Looking at the Fifth from this point of view, we
see that the nearest important consonant intervals
to it are the Fourth and Sixth—both of which differ
from it by a whole tone. The Minor Sixth is of
course still closer to it, but is such a very imperfect
consonance that its proximity hardly affects the consonance of the Fifth. The Fifth is perceptibly rougher
than the Octave only when the upper partials are so
prominent as to give a comparatively harsh quality
of tone. What disagreeable beating there is occurs
chiefly between the fourth and fifth partials of the
one series and the third of the other. Writing the
first six partials of the lower note and the first four
of the upper we have

The single lines indicate pairs of partials at the
interval of a tone. Next in order of consonance

comes the Fourth. This is perceptibly rougher than the Fifth. Within a tone of it on one side is the Fifth and within a semitone on the other side is the

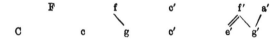

Major Third, so that it may be regarded as either of these intervals mistuned, and our general rule would lead us to expect roughness. On the other hand it is the inversion, i.e. the defect from the Octave, of a Fifth, and no doubt it is partly to this fact it owes its importance. As we see there is beating at the interval of a tone between second and third partials, between fourth and sixth, and between fifth and sixth. There is also beating at the interval of a semitone between fourth and fifth partials as is indicated by the double line.

It is unnecessary to carry this discussion further in detail as no new principles emerge. Indeed we have already discussed all the intervals which were at one time allowed to be consonances at all. The Major and Minor Thirds and the Major and Minor Sixths have now fought their way to a place on the list. Of these the interval with the weakest claim is probably the Minor Sixth, although the fact that it is the inversion of the Major Third is a point in its favour. Obviously the question as to where the list shall close is one which physics can never settle. It is a matter of taste and education. All that physics can do is to explain the reason of dissonance and to arrange the different intervals in order of consonance. It is then open to different nations at different times to draw the line where they please.

Helmholtz classifies consonant intervals as follows:

Absolute Consonances. The Octave, the Twelfth and the Double Octave.

Perfect Consonances. The Fourth and Fifth. These are so called because they may be used in any part of the scale without important disturbance of harmoniousness.

Medial Consonances. The Major Third and Major Sixth. These are distinctly dissonant if used in the lower part of the scale but in the higher part of the scale they are comparatively smooth owing to the rapidity of their beats. They are sharply defined.

Imperfect Consonances. The Minor Third and Minor Sixth. The partials which define these are usually very weak or altogether absent, and but for their importance as inversions of the Major Sixth and Major Third respectively they would hardly occupy the position they do.

It is important to notice that increasing a given interval by an Octave has a very marked effect on its degree of consonance—an effect which cannot be predicted without an examination of the intervals involved. Thus the Fifth becomes the Twelfth and

so passes into the category of absolute consonances.
This is exactly the kind of change that seems reasonable and one might be tempted to expect it in all
cases. The Major Third is also improved and this
seems to bear out our expectations. On the other
hand the Fourth and Major Sixth both become much
more dissonant, being brought very close to the
absolute consonance of the Twelfth. The Figure

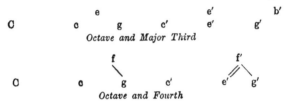

shows the beating intervals in the case of the Octave
and Third and in the case of the Octave and Fourth.
There is no beating in the first case but very marked
beating in the second, especially between the prime
of the one note and the third partial of the other.

From what has preceded it will be evident that
it is impossible to discuss the consonance of intervals
without making specific assumptions as to the number
and prominence of the partials constituting the two
notes. The preceding discussion applies only to the
case—represented fairly accurately by the piano,
harmonium, violin and human voice—where the first
six partials form a series of diminishing importance

and the remaining ones are either altogether absent or very feeble. On the other hand feebly blown stopped organ pipes give very nearly simple tones and with these the Minor Sixth gives quite a smooth impression; other intervals not allowed as consonances at all, although they sound strange and unfamiliar, are not dissonant.

An interesting special case is that of the narrow stopped organ pipe or clarionet, both of which carry the odd members of the series of partials only. Here the dissonance of the various intervals is diminished in a very marked way, and the explanation will be readily grasped if the principles laid down earlier in this chapter are applied to a discussion of the consonance of intervals for this special case.

Another case of interest is that of intervals given on different instruments and so with notes of different quality. When this is the case it may make all the difference to the harmoniousness of the interval which instrument is selected for the lower note. Consider for instance a Major Third given by oboe and clarionet. The oboe gives the full series of

Oboe	C		c	g	c′	c′	g′
Clarionet		E			b		g′♯

Clarionet	C			g		c′	
Oboe		E	e		b	c′	

partials, the clarionet only the odd members of the series.   Take first the case where the lower note is assigned to the oboe.   Here we have two semitone beating intervals.   If, on the other hand, we assign the lower note to the clarionet we find that there

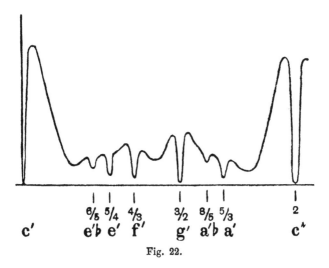

Fig. 22.

are no intervals at all which beat, and the gain in harmoniousness is unmistakable.

Fig. 22 is a graphical representation of the changes in dissonance which take place when the interval between two notes is gradually altered.   If both are originally tuned to c′ and then, while one is kept at that pitch the other be gradually raised to c″, we shall have the conditions represented in the diagram. The distance of the curve from the axis at any point shows the amount of dissonance calculated on certain assumptions when the upper note is tuned to the pitch represented by the point in question. We see that all the well known intervals are represented by dips of the curve and are more or less closely bounded by strong dissonance.

A fuller discussion of consonant intervals under varying circumstances brings out many interesting points but merely requires the application of principles and methods already developed. It lies beyond the scope of this manual and the reader who desires to pursue it is referred to Helmholtz' large work on Sensations of Tone.

CHAPTER VIII

COMBINATION TONES—FURTHER DISCUSSION OF CONSONANT INTERVALS—CONSONANT TRIADS

WHEN it is remembered that almost all musical notes carry with them a number of partial tones, some idea of the complexity of the sensation which is produced when two notes are sounded together is borne in upon the mind. Yet this view of the complexity falls far short of the reality. We have so far left entirely out of account a series of tones known as Combination Tones which undoubtedly play some part in our sensations. These tones were first discovered by the organist Sorge about 1745 but afterwards became known through the Italian violinist Tartini and were called Tartini's tones. They are produced when two pure tones are strongly sounded together. The most important type, the one discovered by Sorge and Tartini, is known as the Differential Tone from the fact that its frequency is equal to the difference of frequencies of the two generating notes. There is also a Summational Tone, whose frequency is the sum of the frequencies of the two generators. This tone is much fainter than the Differential Tone and was not discovered till much later. Both these tones are known as First Order Combination Tones to distinguish them from those of higher orders. These latter are given by one of the generators with one of the Combination Tones. Thus the Second Order Tones are generated by one of the generators and one of the First Order Tones, and so on.

Starting with the most important of the series— the First Order Difference Tone—it will be remarked that its frequency is exactly equal to the number of beats produced between the two generating tones. It is not surprising therefore that the production of these notes has been held to be due to the

coalescence of beats to produce a musical tone. Koenig
held this view and called these tones beat-tones.
Now if this view were established the hypothesis
advanced in the last chapter to account for the
action of the ear must be reconsidered.   In the
first place Combination Tones can be generated by
pure tones separated by the interval of an Octave,
whereas we have given reasons for supposing that
beats cannot occur between pure tones separated
by an interval much greater than a Minor Third.
Further, suppose the generating tones to be c'' and
$e''\flat$—their frequencies are 512 and 614·4. The difference tone has therefore a frequency of about 102
and so must act on the resonators of about this pitch.
On the other hand we have assumed the beats to be
effective on the resonators lying between the two
notes in pitch, i.e. in the neighbourhood of 560.   But
in the form in which we have stated it Koenig's
hypothesis will not bear consideration and by no
manipulation can the phenomena of Combination
Tones be reduced to cases of beats.   To begin with,
they entirely fail to explain the existence of the
summation tones.   The refuge from this objection
which Koenig sought—a denial of their existence—
is no longer open, since their existence is established
beyond question.   In the second place beats can be
heard when two quite faint tones are sounded together, but combination tones only occur when the

two generators are sounded strongly. Perhaps the most interesting fact bearing on the discussion is that the mathematical theory of large vibrations demands the existence of these combination tones whenever the amplitudes of vibration are large. If a vibrating system has imposed on it two sets of vibrations so large in amplitude that the resultant displacement of the system cannot be regarded simply as the sum of the individual displacements, then there appear as components vibrations of the above frequency. Thus if the frequencies of the generating tones are m and n we shall have the following:

First Order Difference Tone $m - n$

First Order Summation Tone $m + n$

Second Order Difference Tones $m - 2n, \ m, \ n$

Second Order Summation Tones $2m - n, \ 2m + n,$ $m + 2n$

and so on. Sometimes these tones can be reinforced by the use of a Helmholtz resonator but in many cases the intensity of the sensation produced in the ear does not seem to be appreciably increased in this way. If the two tones are produced by the same instrument, then some part of the instrument may be the source of the combination tones produced. This is the case for instance when two notes are

sounded together strongly on the harmonium. The
air in the wind-chest is probably the source in this
case and the tones are clearly heard even without
a resonator, but are greatly strengthened when one is
used. Again the air traversed by the two sets of
sound waves on their way to the ear may give rise to
the combination tones, in which case again the use of
a resonator would reinforce them. The amplitude of
the air is rarely sufficient for this. Probably the
commonest case of all is that in which the combination tones are generated in the mechanism of the ear
itself—perhaps in the drum of the ear—and it is
obvious that in this case no resonator can be expected
to reinforce them. For a long time their objectivity
was questioned but it has now been put beyond a
doubt.

They can be quite readily heard on a harmonium
if the generating tones are sounded sufficiently
strongly. Their presence is the more easily marked
if the upper of the two generating tones is kept the
same while the lower is made to descend down the
scale. In this way the difference of frequency between
the two generating tones is increased and the pitch
of the difference tone is raised. The opposite motion
of the lower generator and the First Order Difference
Tone makes observation of the latter more easy. A
series of four diads (pairs of notes) is given in the figure
with the corresponding difference tones. The pitch

of these tones is calculated in the following way.
The first diad is a Minor Third. The frequencies of
the generators are therefore 5 : 6. The frequency of
the difference tone will be represented by 1 on the
same scale that the generators are represented by
5 and 6. Now the upper generator is c''' and its
frequency is represented by 6; c'', the octave lower
will therefore have a frequency 3 and the note a
Twelfth below that again—the note f—will have a
frequency 1. The difference tone in this case is

therefore f. In the second diad we have a Major
Third, c''' being represented by 5 on the same scale
that a'''♭ is represented by 4 and the difference tone
by 1. From this it will be seen that a''♭ is 2 and
therefore a'♭ is 1. The remaining two may be worked
out in the same way. These tones may also be
obtained on the pianoforte but are harder to hear.
To get the summation tone on the harmonium, sound
first the note c and then add to it the note F. The
frequencies of these are in the ratio of 3 : 2. The
frequency of the summation tone will therefore be

represented by 5 on the same scale. It is therefore
a Major Sixth above c and so is the note a. The
existence of the tone will be more easily detected if
the note a is sounded softly first as a guide to the ear
what to expect. The existence of the same summation tone may be recognised in a similar way on the
piano although with more difficulty. The principle of
resonance may be called in to establish its presence.
If the key corresponding to a is depressed while the
two generating tones are strongly sounded two or
three times, then when the sound of the generators
has ceased the note a will be heard sounding. As a
is not a partial of either of the generators this must
be due to the summation tone.

The clearest demonstration of all is probably that
given by a double whistle such as is frequently used
by the police and by referees in football matches.
These consist of two short pipes side by side giving
tones of slightly different pitch so that the first order
difference tone is much lower in pitch and unmistakable after its existence has once been pointed out.
It is this tone which gives the characteristic quality
to these whistles.

We are now in a position to realise the full complexity of the sensation produced by playing, say a
loud triad. Not only does each note carry with it
a series of partials, but each of the constituent partials
of each of the notes is capable of producing with each

of the others a series of combination tones, some of
which are of merely academic importance but some of
which at least have a distinct bearing on the theory
of consonance and dissonance.

In our discussion of consonant intervals we have
up to this point dealt only with tones of fairly good
musical quality, assuming indeed the presence of the
first six partials in each case.   In the case of pure
tones, however, there can be no beating for intervals
greater than the Minor Third.   Is there in this case
any possibility of the simpler intervals being clearly
defined and hedged in by dissonances on either side?
Of course it is more than likely that, being in the
habit of hearing intervals which are exactly defined
by coincident partials, we may carry over to other
cases, in which they are not so defined, associations
which assist the definition.   In addition to this however, when we include combination tones in our
discussion of consonant intervals, we find that at
least in the case of the simplest intervals they do
assist us in defining them even for pure tones.   In
the first place we find that in the case of notes of
good quality the combination tones add nothing to
the beats already present. This can easily be verified
by taking a particular case.   If for instance we take
the imperfect octave 101 : 200, we get partial tones
from the lower note of frequencies 101, 202, 303, 404,
505, and 606.   The partials of the upper note which

are within beating distance of these are 200, 400, 600. Thus we have three sets of beats, 2, 4, and 6 beats per second respectively. Now the first order difference tone has a frequency 99 and so gives with the lower note 2 beats per second; while the second order tones are 101, which coincides with the lower tone, and 2 which is too low to be a tone at all. On the other hand the first order summation tone is 301 and this gives with either generator a difference tone of the same frequency as the other. Thus with all these tones the only beating is at the rate of 2 beats per second which is one of the sets of beats already present if the notes are of good quality. Thus nothing which has so far been said about the consonance of intervals need be revised. On the other hand what has just been said suggests at least that if the tones were pure the first order differential tone formed by two notes at the interval of an octave would give beats with the lower generator if the interval were at all imperfect. This is one explanation of the beating of an imperfect octave when the constituent tones are pure.

In the case of the Fifth the combination tones are less helpful. Here the first order difference tone is an octave below the lower generator but the second order difference tone, made by the first order tone and the higher generator, coincides with the lower generator and so serves to define the interval. Under favourable conditions beats between these two tones due to imperfect tuning may be heard, but it is obvious that the process cannot be pushed much further, and that for less consonant intervals than the Octave and the Fifth, given by absolutely simple tones, accuracy of tuning must be determined more by memory than by the detection of any actual dissonance or beating. Where tones are not absolutely simple but contain the second partial as well as the prime, most of the important intervals are defined by the differential tones of low order.

Having now found a number of consonant intervals we proceed next to see how these may be built up into chords of three notes or triads. Obviously the test of the harmoniousness of a triad will be that when two consonant intervals are added together the two extreme notes shall then form with one another a third consonant interval. To add the two intervals we may simply add the number of cents in each and then see whether the total number corresponds to a consonant interval. We shall confine ourselves within the limits of the Octave, in which case the intervals at our disposal are Minor Third, Major Third, Fourth, Fifth, and Minor Sixth. The Major Sixth when added to the smallest available interval, the Minor Third, gives the Octave, and so is not included in our list. We may add the intervals as follows:

First Interval	Second Interval	Addition	Resultant Interval
Minor Third	Minor Third	316 + 316 = 632	—
Minor Third	Major Third	316 + 386 = 702	Fifth
Minor Third	Fourth	316 + 498 = 814	Minor Sixth
Minor Third	Fifth	316 + 702 = 1018	—
Minor Third	Minor Sixth	316 + 814 = 1130	—
Major Third	Major Third	386 + 386 = 772	—
Major Third	Fourth	386 + 498 = 884	Major Sixth
Major Third	Fifth	386 + 702 = 1088	—
Fourth	Fourth	498 + 498 = 996	—

Thus we see that the only intervals which we can build up into triads are (1) the Minor Third and Major Third, (2) the Minor Third and Fourth, (3) the Major Third and Fourth. On the other hand each of these may be made to give two slightly different triads according to which of the two intervals is put in the lower position. Thus if we make C the starting point in each case, the first triad may be either C : E : G or C : E♭ : G. In the same way the second may be either C : E♭ : A♭, or C : F : A♭, and the third may be either C : E : A, or C : F : A. Thus there are six consonant triads with C as the lowest note although by thus limiting ourselves to C as the lowest note we are compelled to introduce notes which do not belong to the key of C. This could have been avoided by making some of the triads start from different notes. Let us now look a little more closely at the two triads built up from the Major and Minor Thirds. Taking first the triad C : E : G, we see that

if the C be transposed an Octave higher we have
E : G : c.   This triad is said to be an inversion of
the first.   The intervals of which it is now composed
are a Minor Third and a Fourth, so that it is identical
with the triad C:E♭:A♭.   If instead of this particular
inversion we had taken the G of our first triad an
Octave lower we should have had the triad G₁ : C : E.
This is also said to be an inversion of the first triad
and we see that it gives us a triad which is built up
of a Fourth and a Major Third.   It is thus the same
as C : F : A.   Dealing in a similar way with the
second triad C : E♭ : G, we shall find that its inversions
give triads having the same arrangement of intervals
as C : F : A♭, and C : E : A.   Thus the last four triads
can be formed from the first two by inversions, and
so the first two are called fundamental triads.   The
triad C : E : G in which the Major Third comes first
is called the fundamental major triad while the one
in which the Minor Third comes first—C : E♭ : G—
is called the fundamental minor triad.   Putting these
results in staff notation we see that the positions of
the major triad and minor triad are given below.

Major triad.   Minor triad.

It is a well-known fact that the three positions

of the major triad given here are not all equally
harmonious. It will be a useful exercise in the
application of the principles developed in this chapter
if we try to find the reason of this by examining the
possibilities of beating between the partials.

The figure shows the possibilities of beating and we
see that we get semitone beating between partials of
order 3, 4; 4, 5, and 5, 6; also tone beating for 3, 4;
3, 4, and 3, 5. Let us compare this with the second
position. Here we have

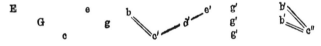

that is semitone beating for partials 2, 3; 3, 5, and
4, 5; also tone beating for partials 2, 3, and 3, 4.
Thus the pairs of partials giving both the tone and
semitone beating in this case are of lower order than
in the first position and therefore correspondingly
more powerful. This position ought therefore to be
less harmonious—a conclusion which accords with
experience. If we compare the first and third
positions in the same way we shall find that there is
little to choose between them, although Helmholtz

puts the third first in order of tunefulness—at least for true intonation. The Minor triads lend themselves to discussion in a similar way, but we shall content ourselves here with a comparison of the major and minor triads. There seems at first sight to be no reason why the fundamental major and minor triads should differ in the impression which they make upon us. They are composed of the same intervals interchanged in relative position; yet there is no doubt that there is a very marked difference in the character of the sensation which they excite. The Minor triad gives an impression, perhaps of greater roughness, certainly of mystery and vague mournfulness. There seems to be nothing in the arrangement of the partials to explain this, but if we take the combination tones into account we at once find the explanation. Considering the fundamental positions only and writing the difference tones due to primes as crotchets and those between primes and second partials as quavers or semi-quavers according to their importance we get the following. For the major triad we may take the frequencies of the primes to be 4, 5, and 6 and therefore those of the second partials as 8, 10, and 12. These give us

(1)   Difference tones between primes,

$$6 - 5 = 1, \qquad 5 - 4 = 1, \qquad 6 - 4 = 2.$$

(2) Difference tones between primes and second partials

$$12 - 6 = 6, \qquad 10 - 6 = 4, \qquad 8 - 6 = 2,$$
$$12 - 5 = 7, \qquad 10 - 4 = 6, \qquad 8 - 5 = 3,$$
$$12 - 4 = 8.$$

Thus on the same scale on which the primes are represented by 4, 5, and 6 the combination tones are represented by 1, 2, 3, 4, 6, 7, and 8. Of these 1 and 2 are much the most important being formed by the

primes. Next to these come 3 and 4 and after these, and still less prominent because given by generators separated by a considerable interval, come the frequencies 6, 7 and 8. Looking either at the numbers or at the notes in the staff notation which they may be taken to represent, we see that all the combination tones, with the single exception of one of the weakest, are octaves of the primes. Passing now to the fundamental minor triad we take as the frequencies $10 : 12 : 15$. These notes give us

(1) Combination tones between primes

$$15 - 12 = 3, \qquad 15 - 10 = 5, \qquad 12 - 10 = 2.$$

(2) Combination tones between primes and second partials

$$30 - 12 = 18, \qquad 24 - 15 = 9, \qquad 20 - 15 = 5,$$
$$30 - 10 = 20, \qquad 24 - 10 = 14, \qquad 20 - 12 = 8.$$

Thus the combination tones have frequencies represented by 2, 3, 5, 8, 9, 14, 18. Showing these in staff notation as before we see that the relation between the combination tones and the primes is

this time entirely different. Here the differential tone introduced by the two primes 12 and 10 gives a note a♭, foreign to the chord, and this note is repeated two octaves higher in the next group. In this group also another new note b♭, makes it appearance to be repeated in the last group an octave higher with a third new note g♭. There is little doubt that it is this absence of close relationship between primes and the combination tones which gives the minor triad its characteristic quality.

CHAPTER IX

DEVELOPMENT OF THE SCALE—TEMPERAMENT

THE music of different nations shows many striking
and characteristic differences, but one fundamental
underlying similarity is at once apparent. Each
nation limits itself to a definite scale or series of
notes and its music proceeds from note to note by
determinate steps and not by slow gliding. It has
been aptly said that music produces its impression
by changes of pitch in time, and of course if these are
to be properly appreciated we must have some units
in terms of which we can measure the two quantities
involved. Rhythm supplies this need for the measurement of time and musical intervals are necessary for
the measurement of changes of pitch. When we
come to examine the selections of notes which the
various nations have made we find them infinitely
varied in detail although certain broad principles are
seen to have influenced the development in all cases.
We find that the Octave is an interval universally
used and that the Fifth and Fourth are extremely
common. Now it will be remembered that these
intervals are the ones which give the most perfect
consonances and if we think of music as we know it
to-day we shall be tempted to conclude that the notes

of the scale were chosen so that they might be used
for harmony. This conclusion however will not bear
consideration. One of the most surprising features
in the history of musical development is the very
late appearance and very slow growth of harmony.
Incredible as it may seem, it is nevertheless true that
as late as the fifteenth and sixteenth centuries the
principles of harmony were unknown and the art
of simple "vamping" still undiscovered. We have
already seen, however, that not only do these intervals
give consonances, but the notes forming them if they
carry series of partials with them are related to
one another by the possession of certain of these
in common. This relationship is less close for the
Fifth than for the Octave and less close for the Fourth
than for the Fifth. In view of this it is at first sight
a little puzzling to find that in some scales the Fourth
is more prominent than the Fifth. This is most
probably to be explained by the consideration that
the note which is the Fourth in the ascending scale
is the Fifth in the descending scale, and that in
melodic music it is quite as natural to think of the
scale as developed downwards as to think of it—as
we are accustomed to do—as developed upwards.
There still remains the difficulty of pure tones, but
these are so rare that it is easy to see that the
development of the scale would be mainly influenced
by notes carrying a fair number of partials.

The diatonic scale is developed from one of the old Greek scales and subsequently modified by the principle of tonality. The Greek scales were developed with the aid of the tetrachord—a four-stringed instrument as its name implies—at first only one being used and then, later, another being added alongside so as to give a series of eight notes. The absence of harmony made these scales somewhat vague and indefinite, and this vagueness was further increased by the absence of any note corresponding to a keynote or tonic. There does indeed seem to have been one note in each scale to which convention attributed a more or less arbitrary importance, but the idea of having one particular note from which a composition should start and to which it should return—a note to which all the notes used in the composition should be more or less closely related—was unknown. This is the principle which gives unity and intelligibility to modern music, and the fact that ancient music did not grasp the need of anything of the kind may have been due to the secondary importance of music as an art—its main function in the earlier stages of its development being that of an accompaniment or setting. We may summarise the achievements of the Greeks in this respect in the words of Professor Sir Hubert Parry. "The Greek system may therefore be considered to have arrived at its complete maturity in the stage in which a range of sounds extending

only for two Octaves was mapped out into a series
of seven modes which can be fairly imitated on a
modern pianoforte by playing the several scales which
begin respectively on E, F, G, A, B, C and D without
using any of the black keys. The difference between
one and another obviously lies in the way in which
the tones and semitones are grouped, and the device
affords considerable opportunity for melodic variety."

During the predominance of purely melodic, or
homophonic music, further important development
was probably impossible; but various influences were
at work which finally carried the art through a
transition stage of polyphonic music to our modern
harmonic type. The natural differences in voices no
doubt contributed. All the male voices of a given
group could not sing the same notes without putting
a strain on the highest pitched voices or the lowest
pitched voices—or on both. This led to the repetition
of the melody a Fifth above or a Fourth below—this
giving the most perfect consonances. Early in the
development of polyphonic music came also the dis-
cantus in which two entirely distinct melodies were
manipulated for simultaneous singing—such liberties
being taken with the time and even with the notes as
would avoid serious discord at any point. Occasionally,
if tradition is to be trusted, a somewhat doubtful
song and an ecclesiastical melody were coupled in
this unholy alliance. But the rapid growth of harmony

and tonality was largely due to the Reformation. It was a Protestant principle that the congregation should do its own singing, and the ecclesiastical music of the time was far beyond the reach of any untrained congregation. There grew up therefore a collection of chorales, often consisting of popular melodies, Germanic in origin and showing—apart altogether from their harmonisation—more feeling for tonality than was possessed by the music of the Southern nations. This development was not without its effect inside the Roman Church, and Palestrina was set the task of modifying the ecclesiastical music of the Church along similar lines. Until recently modern Western European music has shown a steady development in the direction of tonality, all the notes of the diatonic scale being more or less closely related to the key-note.

Accepting this principle then, we shall see how it leads to the development of our modern major diatonic scale. We shall regard as related in the first degree all notes which, when carrying a complete series of the lower partials, have one or more in common. It is obvious that the possession of common high partials can have no real meaning for the ear, as even if in a particular case they are actually present their effect is bound to be masked by the prominence of the lower partials. We shall regard as related in the second degree a pair of notes, each of which is

related in the first degree to a third note. Considering
first of all relationship of the first degree we see
that it must exist between any two notes which form
with one another any of the more consonant intervals.
Now the most consonant are the Octave, Fifth, Fourth,
Major Sixth, and Major Third. The Minor Third we
have already found to be very near the beating
distance. If we take C as our starting-point we shall
find that the other notes defined by these intervals
are, in order, c, G, F, A, E, and if the frequency of C
be represented by 1, their frequencies (see Table III)
will be represented by 2, 3/2, 4/3, 5/3, and 5/4 respectively. Putting them in order we get

> C   E   F   G   A   c

The intervals between them, measured in cents (see
Table III) are 386, 112, 204, 182, and 316 respectively.
Of these intervals the first and last are much larger
than the others and yet it is obvious that if in our
endeavours to fill up these gaps we push relationship
of the first degree any further, we are in danger of
getting into the region of the fanciful. Passing now
to relationship of the second degree we shall choose G
as the note through which the relationship is to be
traced. Next to c it is the most closely related to C
and relationship through c would hardly help us at all.
Two notes fairly closely related to G are the Fourth
below and the Major Third above. These will have

frequencies of $3/4 \times 3/2 = 9/8$ and of $5/4 \times 3/2 = 15/8$, respectively. These give us two notes lying in the gaps to be filled so that we may now write our scale with frequencies and with intervals between successive notes measured in cents as follows:

C	D	E	F	G	A	B	c
1	9/8	5/4	4/3	3/2	5/3	15/8	2
	204	182	112	204	182	204	112

This is in fact the major diatonic scale and other scales and modes may be derived by similar methods. As might be expected the last two notes added were always more indeterminate than the others so long as music was melodic. The most distant relationship to C is that of B but this note has acquired a quite new importance. In a sense it owes its position in the scale to its relationship with G but it has developed for itself the role of "leading note." It is impossible to play over the scale of the white notes and stop at B with any satisfaction—it demands c as its sequel. This is only another instance of the development of tonality which explains also the unsatisfactory nature of the impression made on our minds by one of the old Greek scales.

One other method by which the development of the scale has been attempted deserves mention here— that due to Pythagoras. He supposed it derived by starting with C and proceeding by perfect Fifths,

each note reached being brought down one or more
Octaves so that it might lie between C and c. This
gives us first of all a frequency ratio $3/2$, corresponding
to G ; then $3/2 \times 3/2 = 9/4$, which, if brought down an
octave gives us $9/8$ or D; next comes $3/2 \times 9/4 = 27/8$
which if brought down an Octave give us $27/16$,
a note very close to A; and so on. It must be
obvious that this is a much more artificial method
than the one we have followed. The relationship
between D and C through G might be recognised,
but any more distant relationship than this can have
little meaning.

The comparatively modest requirement of seven
notes to the octave, as represented by the scale we
have just developed, has now been extended, and
the number of notes increased to twelve. In ancient
music the intervals of tones and semitones were
differently arranged in the different modes or scales,
and variety could be introduced in this way. By the
time the development of the diatonic scale was
complete those old modes had disappeared, only two
modes, the major and the minor, being at the disposal
of musicians. This made it eminently desirable that
composers should be free to "modulate" into a different
key for the sake of variety and to return again to the
original key. Not only so, but the fact that the
human voice and many other instruments have a
limited compass made it important that the liberty

of choice of a key-note should be extended to any
note of the scale so that one might be chosen of
such absolute pitch as would bring the composition
within the compass of the instrument in view. Now
if we are to be free to start with any note in the
scale and exactly reproduce the intervals of the
original scale we shall find that our seven notes are
quite insufficient. Indeed without taking the desirability of freedom to modulate into account at all, the
desirability of a new note will be apparent if we
consider the intervals which D makes with A and F.
The frequency ratios of these notes are 9/8, 5/3 and
4/3. The interval D to A ought to be a Fifth
with the ratio 3/2 whereas the actual interval is
$5/3 \div 9/8 = 40/27$. Then again the interval D to F
ought to be a Minor Third—6/5—while the actual
interval is $4/3 \div 9/8 = 32/27$. Thus neither of these
intervals would sound at all well. If, on the other
hand, we had a second D whose frequency ratio was
10/9 we should find that it made with A an exact
Fifth and with F an exact Minor Third.

The note most closely connected with the tonic C
is as we have seen the Fifth above it, G, and this
is the tonic of the key which is most frequently
chosen for modulation. Let us see then what notes
would be required if the intervals of our original
scale are to be reproduced with G as starting-point.
We shall find this by raising each note of the

scale of C by a Fifth, by multiplying its frequency by 3/2.

$$9/8 \times 3/2 = 27/16$$
$$5/4 \times 3/2 = 15/8 \quad \text{or B}$$
$$4/3 \times 3/2 = \ 2 \qquad \text{or C}$$
$$3/2 \times 3/2 = \ 9/4, \quad \text{which taken an Octave lower}$$
$$\text{is } 9/8 \text{ or D}$$
$$5/3 \times 3/2 = \ 5/2, \quad \text{which taken an Octave lower}$$
$$\text{is } 5/4 \text{ or E}$$
$$15/8 \times 3/2 = 45/16, \text{which taken an Octave lower}$$
$$\text{is } 45/32.$$

Thus in addition to G we can still make use of B, C, D and E. Instead of A with a frequency of 5/3 we have a note only slightly different whose frequency is 27/16, but instead of F with a frequency of 4/3 we have a note with a frequency 45/32—almost midway between F and G. Now if we are to be compelled to introduce two new notes for each modulation, it is obvious that the total number of notes required in the Octave will be very large. For voices, and to some extent for stringed instruments, this is a matter of no moment, but for keyed instruments it is of the greatest importance. Difficulties connected with the mechanism and the execution increase rapidly with the number of notes and so some sacrifice of true intonation has to be made in order to limit the number of notes. This limitation is demanded also by considerations of simplicity in tuning an instrument and in writing the music. The necessary compromise is termed "temperament" and may be effected in various ways. A glance at the keyboard of the piano will show that our modern system of temperament is based on a limitation of the notes in the octave to twelve. That this does involve a departure from true intonation may be readily shown. If we ascend twelve Fifths on the piano we find that we have played each note of the Octave once and have ascended seven octaves. Twelve tempered Fifths are thus equal to seven Octaves. But twelve true Fifths are equal to $12 \times 702 = 8424$ cents, whereas seven Octaves are equal to $7 \times 1200 = 8400$ cents. There is therefore an error of 24 cents distributed over twelve Fifths. Similarly three tempered Major Thirds are equal to an Octave. But three true Major Thirds are equal to $3 \times 386 = 1158$ cents while the true octave is of course 1200 cents. An error of 42 cents is therefore distributed between three Major Thirds. The compromise might possibly be avoided by admitting narrower limits of modulation and keeping the intonation true, but it is very doubtful whether in the long run this would be an advantage. There can be no doubt that confining ourselves to tempered intonation involves a real sacrifice. It is foolish to attempt to deny this. No one who has heard the

fundamental major triad successively in true and in
tempered notation can have the least doubt that the
sacrifice is a real one. But the extended possibilities
of modulation is a real advantage and there seems
little prospect of it being abandoned in favour of
more correct intonation.

Many different methods of temperament have
been suggested and tried. Of these only two—
Mean Tone Temperament and Equal Temperament
—need concern us here, although the Pythagorean
is of considerable theoretical interest. In this method
the notes required were obtained by a series of ascending and descending Fifths. These may be written
thus :

C G D A E B F♯ C♯ G♯ D♯ A♯ E♯ B♯ Fx Cx Gx
C F B♭ E♭ A♭ D♭ G♭ C♭ F♭ B♭♭ E♭♭ A♭♭

This system requires 27 notes to the Octave. Its
symbols still linger on in our modern staff notation,
but the system has long since disappeared except in
so far as it may be said to be used by violinists,
whose strings are tuned in a series of perfect Fifths.
The fatal defect of the system for harmonic purposes
is the serious error of the Major Thirds. It will
readily be seen that the Pythagorean Major Third
is four Fifths less two Octaves, or in cents

$$(4 \times 702) - (2 \times 1200) = 408.$$

The true Major Third on the other hand is 386 cents and this sharpening of the Major Third by 22 cents is intolerable in harmonic music.

Coming now to Mean Tone temperament—which takes its name from the fact that it abolishes the distinction between the large and small tones—we find that its Fifths are bad and the facilities for modulation small so long as the number of notes in the octave is limited to twelve. We have already seen that if we ascend by four perfect Fifths and then descend two Octaves we get the Pythagorean Major Third, 22 cents sharp. If, on the other hand, we flatten each of our ascending Fifths by 5·5 cents then, on descending two Octaves we get a true Major Third. Thus the Fifths are appreciably mistuned in order to keep the Thirds true. For perfect freedom to modulate, this system would require 21 notes to the Octave. Nevertheless it prevailed all over the Continent and in England for centuries and only finally disappeared from our pianoforte about 1850. It is probably the best for harmonic purposes.

We come next to consider the now universally adopted system of Equal Temperament. In this system the octave is divided into twelve exactly equal semitones. Two things follow at once. In the first place the number of notes in the Octave satisfies the demand for convenience and in the second place there is complete freedom of modulation. All the intervals being exactly alike it is a matter of convenience which note is chosen as the key-note or starting-point. Rewriting the ascending and descending series of Fifths from C and reversing the order of the notes obtained by descending Fifths we get the series

C G D A E B F♯ C♯ G♯ D♯ A♯ E♯ B♯

D♭♭ A♭♭ E♭♭ B♭♭ F♭ C♭ G♭ D♭ A♭ E♭ B♭ F C

B♯ is, as we have seen, twelve Fifths less seven Octaves, or 24 cents, above C. Obviously then if each of the ascending Fifths had been flattened by two cents the resulting B would have coincided with C. If, similarly, each of the descending Fifths had been flattened by two cents then D♭♭ would have coincided with C. In this case each note of the upper row becomes coincident with the corresponding note of the lower row, so that for practical purposes the distinction between F♯ and G♭, C♯ and D♭ &c. disappears, and we are left with twelve notes in the octave. If we put the comparison of the true intonation with the two latter systems of temperament in tabular form we get the following table which is taken from Barton's *Text-book of Sound.*

The table indicates a clear superiority of the Mean-Tone system over Equal Temperament in the intonation of Major Thirds and Sixths and a not very marked inferiority in the intonation of Fifths.

Against this must be set the superior position of
Equal Temperament in the freedom to modulate
which it confers.

| Notes | Intervals above C and errors of Tempered notes | | | | | |
| | Just Intonation | | Mean-Tone | | Equal Temperament | |
	Frequency Ratios	Cents	Intervals Cents	Errors Cents	Errors Cents	Intervals Cents
C	1	0	0	0	0	0
D	9 : 8	204	193	11	4	200
E	5 : 4	386	386	0	14	400
F	4 : 3	498	503	5	2	500
G	3 : 2	702	697	5	2	700
A	5 : 3	884	890	5	16	900
B	15 : 8	1088	1083	5	12	1100
C	2 : 1	1200	1200	0	0	1200

Some reference ought probably to be made at
this point to a question which has been the subject
of much dispute. It has often been asserted that the
key in which music is written and played gives to
the composition a specific character and that certain
keys are more appropriate than others for compositions of certain kinds. This assertion will carry
a good deal of conviction to the mind of anyone who
tries to execute the same piece of music first in the
key of C major and then in the key of D♭ major.

As performed in C it seems brighter, as performed in
D♭ it sounds softer and more harmonious. It will be
readily agreed that the explanation is not to be found
merely in the difference of pitch in the two cases.
This has been verified by tuning one piano a semitone
below another. The character of the composition is
found to attach itself to the nominal keynote, and
even if D♭ on the first piano be tuned to C on the
second, a piece of music played in D♭ on the first
piano sounds appreciably softer than the same piece
performed in C on the second piano. If our keys—
like the old tonal modes—had a different distribution
of the tones and semitones, a difference of character
would be explicable. The difference in character of
music in our major and minor modes respectively
is undoubtedly partly attributable to this cause.
Between the various major keys however there is
no distinction of this kind—tones and semitones are
distributed in the same order in all of them. Indeed,
if the tuning process has been carried out so as to
give exactly equal temperament, then playing the
same composition in different keys simply means
playing it at different pitches. Some light is thrown
on the subject if we consider how far these supposed
differences of character depend on the particular
instrument on which the composition is executed.
Most impartial observers seem to be agreed that on
the organ they are altogether absent. This of course

suggests that the explanation is to be found in the particular mechanism of the piano and may be due to the different action of the black and white digitals respectively. It stands to reason that whatever the mechanism may be, it must be extremely difficult to produce identically the same effect as regards time of contact, force, displacement, &c., where the two levers which start the action are of different lengths. The black and white digitals are differently distributed in different keys and of course the black digitals are much used in the key of D♭ and not at all in the key of C except as accidentals. In some other types of musical instruments similar differences are found. For instance in stringed instruments notes produced on the open string have quite a different quality from those produced by stopping. Keys in which frequent use of these open notes is made may well differ in character from those in which their use is less frequent. Not only so, but the system of tuning stringed instruments does not give equal temperament, as the open strings are tuned in a series of true Fifths. Similar arguments apply to some of the wind instruments and so we see that in the case of many musical instruments there are differences which might be supposed to account for the existence of the differences of character under discussion. On the other hand no explanation has been given, apart from particular instruments, and in the case of the organ, for example, no explanation along these lines can be attempted.

A more extreme claim still is sometimes made—the claim that a piece of music sounds different according as it is played in D♭ or in C♯. Here, in instruments tuned in equal temperament, exactly the same succession of notes is played, and this fact suggests that, in the minds of some enthusiasts at least, association of ideas plays a larger part in the phenomenon than is commonly admitted. A key is probably associated mentally with one or more familiar compositions written in that key, and the characteristics of these compositions are then instinctively transferred to the key itself.

CHAPTER X

MUSICAL INSTRUMENTS

FROM many points of view, the most important class of musical instruments is that in which the sound waves in the air take their origin from the vibrations of a stretched string or wire. The vibrations are excited by bowing, by striking with a hammer or by plucking, and are usually reinforced by being communicated to some extended surface, so that a large mass of air may be set in vibration.

Typical of the group of stringed instruments where the vibrations are excited by a bow is the violin, and we shall consider it first. Its essential features are well known. The body of the instrument is a shallow box, oblong in shape and with somewhat convex top and bottom. From one end of this box projects the handle of the instrument, which carries the pegs (to which the strings are attached) and a finger-board without frets. To the other end of the body is attached a tail-piece into which the other ends of the strings are fixed. The strings pass over a small wooden bridge which rests on the upper side or belly of the instrument and is kept in position by the pressure of the stretched strings. The four strings are tuned in perfect fifths by adjusting the tension by means of the pegs, and are made to give the various notes of the scale by "stopping"—i.e. by pressing them with the finger down on to the finger-board—and so shortening their vibrating length. The absence of frets gives perfect freedom to the performer, who can play in true intonation if desired. On the other hand, it gives no assistance whatever to the novice in the matter of correct intonation. As shortening the string must always raise the pitch of the note, it is obvious that the compass of the violin is limited at the lower end by the prime tone of the lowest string. The upper limit depends almost solely on the skill of the performer. In addition to the high notes obtained by stopping in the ordinary way, other notes, known as harmonics, may be obtained by touching the string lightly at various points (see page 74). Thus touching it at a fourth of its length from one end makes it split up into four vibrating sections, and so gives the double octave of its prime tone. The special quality of tone characteristic of the violin is associated with a very complete set of partial tones, the presence of these being due to the lightness and flexibility of the strings. The so-called cat-gut of which these are made is obtained from the intestines of lambs. In order to preserve the flexibility in the case of the fourth string and to avoid giving it a thickness appropriate to its low tone, a comparatively thin gut-string is wrapped round with fine wire. This increases the mass of the string per unit length without unduly interfering with its flexibility. The motion of the violin string has been studied by Helmholtz and others. Different points in the vibrating string may be made to reveal their method of vibration by means of a device due to Krigar Menzel and Raps. In their arrangement a brightly illuminated vertical slit is placed behind a horizontally stretched string at the point where the motion is to be observed. An image of this slit is thrown on a photographic plate by a lens, and appears as a bright slit with a dark spot where it is crossed by the string. If now the string is bowed in such a way as to throw it into vibration in a vertical plane, the spot will appear to move up and down, following the motion of the string. If the string is stretched so as to give a note of reasonable pitch, these vibrations will be much too rapid to be visible, but, if the plate is moved horizontally at the same time, a wavy curve will be traced on it which, a moment's consideration will convince us, is in fact the displacement diagram of the point of the string under observation. The diagram so obtained generally shows the straight line type to which reference has already been made, although the form depends to some extent upon the point of observation and the point at which the bow is applied. Thus, in a case where the string was bowed at a point one-third of its length from the end and observed in the middle, it gave an almost smooth simple harmonic curve. This is of course exactly what we should expect. The middle of the string—which is the point under observation—is a node for the second, fourth and sixth partials. The point of trisection of the string— which is the point bowed—must be a node for the third, sixth and ninth partials. Thus we see that the first group of partials will escape observation, while the second group, owing to the bow being applied at the point where they require a node, will be absent. Thus the only important partials which can be observed are the prime and the fifth, and the latter will be comparatively very weak indeed. If we apply to the ordinary straight-line displacement diagram the methods of interpretation suggested on page 31, we shall see that it represents the motion of a point which moves for a time in one direction with constant speed, and then changes its direction and retraces its path again with constant speed. This gives us a little insight into the probable action of the bow on the string. It is a well-known fact that the frictional force between two surfaces is greater when they are relatively at rest than when they are in relative motion. The rosined bow grips the string, pulling it aside until the tension of the string tending to restore it to its undisplaced position overcomes the force of friction. The string then springs back until displaced in the other direction, when it is again gripped by the bow. The bow is usually applied to a point of the string about one-twelfth of the length from the bridge. It is as a rule applied nearer to the bridge in forte passages, and if applied further from the bridge gives a softer and mellower tone. Its motion ought to be across the string. Any motion along the string tends to excite longitudinal vibrations, and these correspond to very shrill and high-pitched notes. It is the accidental occurrence of these longitudinal vibrations which makes the early efforts of the beginner so distressing to hear.

The vibrations of the strings themselves would give a very weak and poor tone if they were unable to communicate their vibrations to a resonant surface of some kind. This is achieved by the bridge which transmits the vibrations of the strings to the belly of the instrument. The foot of the bridge under the first string takes little part in this transmission. The sound-post—which connects the belly and the back and sustains the pressure of the bridge—touches the belly at a point close to this foot. The foot of the bridge on the side of the fourth string, however, is subjected to less pressure since this string is less tightly stretched and at the same time the part of the belly with which it is in contact is free to move. This foot therefore plays the principal part in the transmission of the vibrations. These vibrations are then transmitted to the back by the sides, or ribs, and by the sound-post—but mainly by the latter. In addition to the two functions of the sound-post already mentioned it helps to determine the form of vibration of both belly and back of the instrument, as the two points to which it is glued must be nodes.

The tone given by the instrument as a whole seems to depend upon the wood chosen, the shape and the varnish. Mere antiquity confers no special virtue on a violin but the best of the old violins are undoubtedly superior to those of the present day, and no important advance in the construction of the

instrument has been made during the last 150 years.
It is difficult to fix on any one feature as being the
probable cause of the superiority of the old instruments, but the records which have come down to us
show that the choice, application, and drying of the
varnish occupied a good deal of the attention of the
old makers.

A great deal of what has been said with regard
to the violin may be applied with modifications to
other stringed instruments.   In the piano of course
the strings are set in vibration by blows from
hammers actuated by keys.   There is a separate
key, hammer and, usually, a pair of strings for each
note in the range of the instrument.   The quality
depends mainly on the point on the strings which
the hammers are made to strike, on the hardness of
the hammers, on their time of contact with the strings,
and on the sounding board.   The point of attack
on the strings is usually selected so as to make the
seventh, eighth, and ninth partials very weak.   The
sharper and harder the hammer surface is, the more
abrupt is the displacement of the string and the
more prominent are the upper partials.   Thus hard,
sharp hammers give a quality which is brilliant and
even harsh, while soft flat hammers tend to dulness
of tone.   The hammers are usually faced with compressed felt and if the tone is too brilliant it can be
softened down to any extent by teasing out the felt.

Similar considerations apply to instruments where the string is excited by plucking. A broad, soft plucking instrument, e.g. the finger, as used in the harp, gives a sweet and soft tone ; while the ivory plectrum as used in the mandoline gives a harsh, metallic quality of tone.

Passing next from stringed instruments to wind instruments, we may consider first of all the organ, which may be taken as typical of instruments which depend on the vibrations of a column of air. It is an instrument which gives the performer an un-rivalled control of musical effects both as regards single qualities of tone and combinations of these. The pipes are arranged in ranks and are controlled by stops and keys. Each stop is practically a separate musical instrument, and when a particular stop is in use, all the notes of the key-board or manual give notes similar in quality. The differences in quality corresponding to different stops are produced by series of pipes modified in various ways. Thus pipes are divided into two great classes—flue pipes, where the vibration of the air in the pipes is caused directly by the air-blast from the bellows striking the lip ; and reed pipes where the blast sets in motion a thin metallic strip which by periodically interfering with the blast sets the air in the pipe into vibration. Flue pipes may be made of wood—in which case they are usually rectangular in section—or of metal—in which

case they are usually circular in section. Wooden
pipes give a distinctly mellower quality of tone than
metal ones. Again, flue pipes may be either open or
stopped—i.e. closed at the upper end. Open pipes
as we have seen carry the complete series of lower

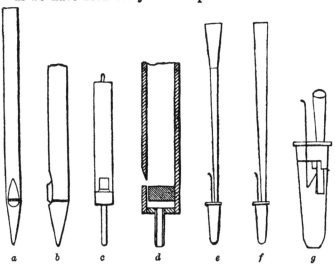

Fig. 23.   (a) (b) Open diapason, (c) (d) Stopped diapason, (e) Oboe
(reed), (f) Trumpet (reed), (g) Reed mouthpiece.

partials, while stopped pipes carry only the odd
members of the series. This gives a distinctive
difference in quality between the two classes of flue
pipes. The various notes of the scale are got by

using pipes of various lengths and the tuning to the
exact pitch necessary may be achieved in a variety
of ways. The tone of the open pipe may be flattened
by partially shading the end with a leaden strip and
sharpened by slightly opening a hole in the side of
the pipe a short distance from the end. The tone of
the closed pipe can be tuned by adjusting the stopper.

Reed pipes give a more cutting quality of tone,
and this is especially the case for beating reeds. In
these the reed is larger than the opening over which
it vibrates, and so the edges of the reed strike the
edges of the opening at each vibration. In this way
the cutting off of the air-blast is made more sudden
and more complete. To avoid a disagreeable harshness the reed is curved and made to roll over the
opening, the lower end of the reed closing over the
aperture before the tip, thus making the stoppage of
the air-blast more gradual. Reed pipes are, as a rule,
conical or pyramidal in shape, the wide end being at the
top. In all cases the quality is duller and softer for
pipes of large cross-section and richer and brighter for
pipes of small cross-section. In the case of stopped flue
pipes and even open flue pipes if the cross-section
is considerable, "mixture" stops are used coupling
with each pipe a series of others which reinforce
its lower partials. The quality of tone given by a
particular pipe is considerably affected by the shape
of the lip and its position relative to the slit through

which the air comes. The adjustment of this position
is called "voicing." The reed is tuned by means of
a small wire with a cross-piece which slides over the
reed, clamping it against the side of the pipe. This
wire can be pushed up or down and so may be made
to shorten or lengthen the free part of the reed (see
Fig. 23 (*g*)).

Another very important class of instruments which
depend on the vibrations of air columns is that com-
prising the wind instruments of the orchestra. Some,
as for example the flute, are special adaptations of the
flue pipe of the organ, the mode of vibration of the
air in the pipe and pitch of the resulting tone being
controlled by opening and closing apertures at different points in the pipe. In the brass wind instruments of the orchestra the lips of the performer act
as a double membranous reed and are the controlling
cause of the vibrations of the air in the instrument.
In all instruments of the kind the essential feature is
a brass tube tapering towards the end to which the
mouth is applied and opening out towards the other.
The degree of tapering is carefully adjusted, so that
the natural modes of vibration of the air in the tube
may give a series of partials forming an exact harmonic series with the prime. The tension of the lips
of the performer determines the period of their own
vibrations, and that in turn determines which partial
of the series will be evoked. Only when the frequency

of vibration of the lips coincides with one of the
partials of the instrument will any musical note be
produced. It is clear that this is a very serious
limitation. Thus the prime tone and second partial
are separated by an octave, the second and third
partials by a Fifth, the third and fourth by a Fourth,
and the fourth and fifth by a Major Third. Even
using the higher partials only, the scale is very
incomplete indeed. This necessitates the use of
some device for obtaining intermediate notes if
the instrument is to have much musical value. In
the bugle there is no provision of any kind. The
range of possible tones is confined to the harmonic
series. In the French Horn the possibilities are still
somewhat limited, although the device for obtaining
intermediate notes is fairly effective in the hands of
a skilled performer. Only the higher and therefore
closer partials are used, and intermediate notes are
obtained by thrusting the hand into the bell of the
instrument and so lowering the natural note by a
semitone or even a whole tone. Of course the
character of the tone suffers a little in consequence.
The tuning of the instrument may be altered a
tone by means of a removable "crook." Part of the
tube of the Horn is U-shaped and may be removed
and replaced by a slightly longer crook. In this way
the tuning may be changed from F to E♭. In the
trombone this idea is still further developed, as here

we have a sliding crook which can be adjusted between the execution of two successive notes of a
piece of music. These sliding pieces have seven
positions and a change from one to the next changes
the scale by a semitone, so that the scale of the
instrument may be changed by three complete tones.
This serves to fill all the gaps between the second
and third partials, and, in addition, gives alternative
methods of playing the higher notes which are occasionally useful. On the other hand the clumsiness of
the movement necessary for adjusting the tube makes
the trombone a very unsuitable instrument for the execution of rapid passages. In the trumpet and allied
instruments recourse is had to valves which bring into
action tubes of different lengths. There are, as a rule,
three such valves, depressing the scale of the instrument by a semitone, a tone, and three semitones respectively. As they can be used simultaneously this makes
provision for the depression of the scale of the instrument by six semitones—as in the case of the trombone.
The mechanism here is much easier to manipulate,
but unfortunately subsidiary valves and crooks have
to be added for a reason which will be readily
apparent. Some apparatus must be provided for
tuning the instrument if it is to be used with others.
This takes the form of a small adjustable crook which
may be used to alter the scale by about a semitone.
Now the effect of the addition of a length of tubing

to the original length depends not simply on the length added but on the ratio of this to the original length. Thus if we were to add 20 cms. to a tube whose original length was 20 cms. we should alter its scale by an octave, whereas if the original length of the tube were 40 cms. we should only alter its scale by the interval of a Fifth. Thus if the lengths of tube brought into action by the valves give a lowering of the scale by an exact number of semitones for one position of the tuning-crook, they will not do so for another. Then again for a similar reason if the third valve produces a lowering of a tone and a half when used alone, the lowering it produces when used along with one of the other valves will be less than this. In order to give facilities for adjusting the valves for any position of the tuning-crook each of them is fitted with a small slide, and in instruments where the lower notes of the series of harmonics are much used, the second and third valves are provided with compensating valves which come into operation when these valves are used together or in combination with the first.

A brief mention of instruments depending on the vibrations of reeds alone, without associated air columns will be enough. This type is represented by the harmonium, the concertina and the American organ. The fundamental difference between the first and last of these is that in the harmonium the air is

driven through the reeds by the bellows, while in
the American organ the bellows create a partial
vacuum and the pressure of the atmosphere outside
drives air through the reeds to supply it. Considering the harmonium a little more in detail we
find that the notes are given by the vibrations of free
reeds. These are thin metallic strips fixed at one
end. Their natural frequency of vibration will depend
on the ratio of the stiffness to the massiveness (in
technical terms, the ratio of the restoring couple to
the moment of inertia). Filing the free end will
diminish the massiveness without appreciably affecting the stiffness, and so will increase the frequency.
Filing the fixed end will greatly diminish the stiffness
without much affecting the massiveness and so will
diminish the frequency and flatten the tone. The
reeds are tuned in this way and, unlike the piano,
the harmonium only requires very occasional tuning.
Above each reed is a small air-chamber whose shape
and size determines the quality but not the pitch of
the note emitted. Good instruments have eight sets
of these, controlled by stops—four for the treble and
four for the bass. The pressure in the wind-chest is
regulated by a valve which allows the air to escape
into a chamber communicating with the outer air.
A stop called the Expression stop can be used to cut
off this communication and the pressure of the wind
in the wind-chest is then completely controlled by

the pedals and the sound may be made to swell or
diminish at pleasure.

The apparatus by which the human voice produces
musical notes may be classed as a double reed. In
a cavity known as the larynx, situated at the top of
the windpipe and marked in position by the familiar
projection called "Adam's apple," are two horizontal
stretched membranous bands—the vocal cords. In
repose their inner edges meet at a fairly acute angle
while their outer edges are attached to the wall of
the larynx. During deep inspiration they are widely
separated while in the production of sounds their
edges are brought parallel and practically into contact, thus closing the larynx against the passage of
air from the lungs to the mouth and nose. When
a sound is produced these bands are set in vibration
and maintained in vibration by the passage of a
stream of air between their edges. The lungs act as
a kind of bellows, increasing the pressure of the air
below the cords. This pressure drives the edges of
the cords upwards and some air escapes. The pressure is thus reduced and the elasticity of the cords
brings them back into position, the cords being thus
kept vibrating steadily with a frequency determined
mainly by their natural length and their tension. Thus
in men the natural length of these cords is greater
than in women and the familiar phenomenon of the
breaking of a boy's voice is due to the rapid growth

of the larynx and the corresponding increase in the length of the vocal cords. Differences in the quality of the sound produced depend to some extent on the flexibility of these cords and to a large extent also on the shape of the cavities of the mouth, throat and nose. A contrivance known as the laryngoscope enables us to study the vocal cords in action. By means of a mirror held at the back of the throat a powerful beam of light is thrown down into the larynx thus lighting up the mechanism it contains and the reflection of this mechanism in the mirror may then be examined. The vocal cords stand out clearly from their surroundings, being greyish white. It is usual to recognise the division of the human voice into three registers—the low, or chest register, the middle register, and the small, or head register. These have been named by Behnke the thick, thin and small registers respectively to correspond to the method of production of the sound in each case. Thus, according to this observer, the thick register is produced by vibrations of the cords as a whole. In the thin register only the inner edges participate in the vibration, while in the case of the small register the motion is confined to the central portion of the inner edges of the cords.

Much work has been done on the production of vowel sounds by the human voice without any very general agreement being reached. It is well known that to produce any particular vowel sound the mouth and throat cavities must be put into a particular shape, whatever note it is desired that the vowel shall be sung to. It is found that when so placed the mouth and throat reinforce notes of particular pitch as may be found by holding tuning-forks of different frequencies in front of the mouth. Results of this kind suggested the "fixed pitch" theory of vowel production—the theory that when a given vowel is sung to any note whatever, one or more partials of definite pitch, always the same for the same vowel, are reinforced by the mouth and throat cavities. Against this was placed a "relative pitch" theory, which supposed that it was the relation between the upper partials and the prime which was effective in determining the vowel and that when the vowel was sung to a note of higher pitch the whole series of partials rose, the distribution of intensity between them remaining roughly the same. Recent work by Boeke and others seems to suggest that the truth lies between the two views. Apparently when the note to which the vowel is sung is raised, the partial or partials whose prominence is characteristic of the vowel rises too although through a much smaller interval, a rise of one octave in the prime tone being accompanied by a rise of only a semitone or so in the characteristic partial.

Table IV taken from Barton's *Sound* gives a rough idea of the partials given by various instruments and of their relative strengths.

TABLE I

Helmholtz notation as used in the text

C₁   C   c   c′   c″   c‴   cᴵⱽ

The letter denoting any particular note has the same distinguishing mark as the C immediately below it. Thus

c   d   e   f   g   a   b   c′   d′ &c.

TABLE II

Interval	Ratio of Frequencies	Notes within a single octave giving the interval
Octave ...	2 : 1	c : C
Major Sixth	5 : 3	A : C B : D
Minor Sixth	8 : 5	c : E
Fifth ...	3 : 2	G : C B : E c : F
Fourth ...	4 : 3	F : C G : D A : E c : G
Major Third	5 : 4	E : C A : F B : G
Minor Third	6 : 5	G : E c : A

TABLE III

Notes of Scale	C	D	E	F	G	A	B	c
Frequency Ratios	1	$\frac{9}{8}$	$\frac{5}{4}$	$\frac{4}{3}$	$\frac{3}{2}$	$\frac{5}{3}$	$\frac{15}{8}$	2
Frequency Ratios expressed in whole numbers ...	24	27	30	32	36	40	45	48
Intervals between successive notes expressed as ratios		$\frac{9}{8}$	$\frac{10}{9}$	$\frac{16}{15}$	$\frac{9}{8}$	$\frac{10}{9}$	$\frac{9}{8}$	$\frac{16}{15}$
Intervals expressed in cents	204	182	112	204	182	204	112	

Simple Intervals expressed in Cents

Octave ...	1200		Major Third	386
Major Sixth	884		Minor Third	316
Minor Sixth	814		Large Tone	204
Fifth ...	702		Small Tone	182
Fourth ...	498		Semitone	112

BIBLIOGRAPHY

HELMHOLTZ.   Sensations of Tone.   (A detailed non-mathematical treatment.)

BARTON.   Text-Book of Sound.   (An elementary mathematical treatment.)

BOUASSE.   Bases Physiques de la Musique.

Encyclopædia Britannica, Eleventh Edition.   Articles—Ear, Music, Organ, Sound, Violin.

APPENDIX

THE following short account of the logarithmic method of measuring musical intervals is taken from Professor Barton's *Text-Book of Sound.*

"Let the frequencies of three notes, beginning at the highest and proceeding in order of pitch be L, M, and N. Also let the intervals be I_1 between L and M, I_2 between M and N, and I between L and N. Then if each interval be measured by k times the logarithm of the ratio of the frequencies, we have

$$I_1 = k \log \frac{L}{M} = k (\log L - \log M)\ldots\ldots\ldots(1),$$

$$I_2 = k \log \frac{M}{N} = k (\log M - \log N)\ \ldots\ldots(2),$$

$$I = k \log \frac{L}{N} = k (\log L - \log N)\ldots\ldots\ldots(3).$$

But by addition of (1) and (2)

$$I_1 + I_2 = k (\log L - \log N)\ \ \ldots\ldots\ldots(4),$$

so by (3) and (4)

$$I = I_1 + I_2 \ldots\ldots\ldots\ldots\ldots\ldots\ldots(5).$$

For k any convenient number could be chosen, as (5) shows that the relation desired is independent of it. But the late Mr A. J. Ellis (the translator of Helmholtz's *Sensations of Tone*) has adopted as the unit for this logarithmic measure the *cent*, 1200 of which make the octave. The name cent is used because 100 cents make the semitone of those instruments in which twelve equal semitones are the intervals occurring in an octave. Hence the clue to reduction of any intervals to these logarithmic cents would be found in the following equations, where I is the interval in cents between notes of frequencies M and N :—

$$I = k \log \frac{M}{N} \quad \dots\dots\dots\dots(6),$$

$$1200 = k \log 2 \quad \dots\dots\dots\dots(7)$$

Whence by (6) ÷ (7)

$$I = 1200 \, \frac{\log M - \log N}{\log 2} \text{ ,,}$$

TABLE IV. PARTIALS OF TYPICAL INSTRUMENTS

Instruments			Partials and their Relative Intensities								Authorities and Remarks
			1	2	3	4	5	6	7	8	
Harp			100	81·2	56·1	31·6	13	2·8	—	—	Theory of Helmholtz for string plucked at one-seventh
Piano			100	99·7	8·9	2·3	1·2	0·01	—	—	Theory of Helmholtz for string struck at ⅐th and like c″ on his grand piano and experiment
Violin			100	25	11	6	4	3	2	1·5	Helmholtz theory and experiment
Flute Pipes of Organ	Stopped	Wide	X	—	x	—	—	—	—	—	
		Narrow	X	—	X	—	x	—	—	—	Helmholtz theory and experiment
	Open	Wide	X	X	x	—	—	—	—	—	
		Narrow	X	X	X	X	X	x	—	—	
Flute			X	x	X	X	X	X	X	X	(And beyond the 8th for 8 forks cannot match it
Oboe			X	X	X	X	X	X	X	X	Helmholtz and Blaikley
Clarinet			f	—	f	(p)	mf	(p)	mf	(pp.)	
French Horn or Euphonium ...			X	X	X	X	X	X	X	X	
Trumpet or Trombone ...			X	X	X	X	X	X	X	X	
Human voice ...			X	X	X	X	X	X	X	X	(And up to 16th detected by Helmholtz in bass voices

INDEX

9 781107 684621